CLASSIC HOTELS OF THE WORLD:3
CÔTE D'AZUR

PHOTOGRAPHY & TEXT
HIRO KISHIKAWA

SUPERVISION
JIRO HIRASHIMA

KAWADE SHOBO SHINSHA

A postcard dating from 1913. At the end of the nineteenth century the walkway along the beach was called the *Promenade des Anglais* (Walkway of the Englishmen), a casino was constructed on a pier over the water, and Nice's Golden Age was underway.

序　平島 二郎 建築家

　透明な青空にキリリと切りこむ、頂きには白雪を残すアルプスの遠望と、近くはazure「碧」の海と……その海は空の青さを映してさらに青い。第3巻では南フランスCote d'Azurのリゾート・ホテルを紹介する。

　その位置が湾を巻き込む岬の先端に在るため、あたかも海上に浮かぶ船から眺めるように、山と海とを同時に、「シャンパンの泡がはじけるような陽光が降り注ぐ天使の湾岸線」を見渡せるサン・トロペの別荘地。その東には映画祭開催で広く知られるカンヌ市が在り、画家のルノワールが晩年の12年を過ごした邑カーニュもある。さらに東には謝肉祭の一日、ミモザの花束を華やかに投げあう花祭が楽しいニースもある。香水のまちグラースやイタリア国境に近いマントンの地域と、モナコ公国モンテ・カルロを併せて、南仏プロヴァンスの地中海沿岸の此の地は「気候と景観の双方」が共に優れ、加えて宿泊設備が整った一級のリゾートである。

　かつてこの地のかなりの部分がイタリア領土であった歴史を秘めた形で、Rivieraとも呼ばれる。cityは普通名詞だがCityはロンドンの或る地域の固有名詞。と同様にイタリア語の海岸を意味する普通名詞rivieraが特定の地名として此処に使われている。今、我々にとって、ふたつの呼び名のうちコート・ダジュールのほうが、馴染みのある呼び名であろう。

　この地域一帯がコート・ダジュールの名で、まずロンドンの社交界で語られるようになってから、すでに一世紀がたつ。未だこの地がその名前で呼ばれてはいなかった頃、当時イタリア領であったニースへイギリスの貴族ブルーム卿が赴いたのは1834年のこと。この年は、我が国では江戸と大阪で大火があった将軍家斉の時代、欧州では四国(イギリス・フランス・スペイン・ポルトガル)同盟成立の年であり、この前後にギリシアとベルギーが、また南米でもいくつかの国が独立した時代である。

　夏には雨がなく冬季にはある程度の降雨、オリーブのような硬葉樹は成育可能で、草花も美しく育てられるが、年間どちらかといえば乾燥のいわゆる『地中海気候』のなかで、加えて緯度──北海道の稚内あたり──の割にはアルプスが冬の北風を遮るため冬も暖かい。この地方は、その気候特性からひとつの地域に纏められる潜在的な可能性は昔から在ったものの、ブルーム卿が旅行した頃は、ただ海岸に幾つかの寒村が点在する単なるフランスの辺境であった。コート・ダジュールの名のもとにトゥーロンからマントンまでを一体に纏めて見る扱いはなかった。

　この年の2年前にはコレラが欧州で蔓延し、アメリカで初めて発病者が出た年である。また翌1835年には初めてドイツで鉄道が開通した。欧米二大陸間の旅行者数の増大が、コレラが大西洋を越えたことの原因である、とする説の当否は擱いて、初めてドイツにおいて一

部ではあるが鉄道が開通したということ、それは19世紀の前半にすでにヨーロッパでの交通手段が馬車から鉄道に移行し始めたこと、すなわち旅行者数の増大を示している。

ブルーム卿はイギリスからニースに向かう間にカンヌに立ち寄った。卿は人口数千の漁村に魅せられて直ちに別荘を設け、90歳で死ぬまでの34年間、毎年の休暇をこの地で過ごした。初めは霧深いロンドンに住みながら、そこから重い腰を上げなかった英国貴族の多くがやがてカンヌやニースにヴァカンスを過ごすようになり、遂にはヴィクトリア女王もこの地に赴くことになったのは、ブルーム卿のこの地への深い愛情、礼賛の故である。

19世紀の前半、マルセイユ～アヴィニヨン間が開通した1848年頃までのフランスでも、路線はわずかであった。総延長1800～1900kmを16の小企業が細々と分けあっていた。しかし後半になると企業は合併し、著しく発達したのである。

19世紀フランス政治社会史の権威、プロヴァンス大学教授でプロヴァンス歴史協会会長でもある Pierre Guiral ピエール・ギラール教授は、巻末に膨大な参考文献リストをのせた『キャピタリズムの黄金時代1852～1879──フランスに於ける日常生活』の中で、「第2帝政期1857年には同国の鉄道は近隣諸国の路線と繋り、1870年には路線延長18,000kmを6社の大企業が運営するまでに成った。帝政から第三共和制になって、直ちにはその利益が理解し難いが、港湾を近代化し、鉄道の必要な連絡路線を辺鄙な地方まで伸ばすフレシネ計画、一大事業計画（1878～79）が完成し、結果として中央集権化と諸産業の発展を加速した。」と述べている。鉄道を介する革命思想の地方への急速な広がり、聖地巡礼の復活、そして諸産業の発展の内には、農業の発展が著しいという、ちょっと意外な項目が目に付き、また医師などのブルジョワが温泉地の開発とホテル産業に投資して成功した実例や、大資本の観光産業への進出も述べられている。しかし「フランスで最も珍しいものといえば、旅行したことのあるフランス人」というアルフレッド・アソランの一文の引用が見られる。

フランスの夏といえばバカンス、「バカンスは生活習俗であると同時に法律…」という年次有給休暇が認められたのは1936年、レオン・ブルムの左翼人民戦線内閣がフランス雇用者総連合と労働総同盟の間にマチニヨン協定を結ばせ、法制化した結果である。戦後の現在、バカンスに出る人の80％が自動車でフランス国外に行く。そして、コートダ・ジュールは昔ながらの、各国の言葉が入り乱れる国際的な雰囲気を十分に保っている。

Introduction by Jiro Hirashima Architect

Along the shores of the Mediterranean in southern France the open, cloudless sky is azure, with the white peaks of the snow-covered Alps visible in the distance. Azure is also the color of the sea, reflecting the sky above. This volume, number three in the series exploring classic hotels of the world, takes us to the Azure Coast—the Côte d'Azur—to visit the resort hotels there.

One famous vacation spot along the coastline is St. Tropez, with its many summer cottages. Situated on the tip of a cape wrapping around a bay, St. Tropez offers the same view one would get from a boat floating out over the water—mountains in the distance, the sea in the foreground, and "sunlight pouring down over the angelic shoreline like champagne bubbles bursting." To the east is Cannes, scene of the annual film festival, and Cagnes, where the painter Renoir spent twelve years towards the end of his life. Still further to the east is Nice, where bouquets of mimosa blossoms are tossed back and forth during the annual flower festival. Also part of the Côte d'Azur region are the area of Grasse, with its perfume makers; Menton, at the Italian border; and Monte Carlo, in the principality of Monaco. Here along the coast of Provence the pleasant climate, beautiful scenery and excellent lodging facilities have combined to create a world-class resort area.

Surprisingly, a large part of this shoreline was once part of Italy, and the area including the Côte d'Azur has another name—the Riviera. Just as "city" is a common noun but "City" is a proper name referring to the financial district of London, so too "riviera" simply means "seashore" in Italian, but "Riviera" is the proper name for this particular stretch of shore. Of the two names, though, Côte d'Azur is far more familiar to us, so

that is the name we'll use here.

The term "Côte d'Azur" was first used more than a century ago, in London society. It was in 1834, when the area was still under Italian rule, that it was first visited by Lord Bloome, an English aristocrat. In Japan it was the era of the shoguns, and that year saw major fires in Edo (Tokyo) and Osaka. In Europe an alliance had just been formed among the four nations of England, France, Spain and Portugal, and around that time a number of countries were first gaining their independence, including Greece, Belgium, and much of South America.

The climate of the Côte d'Azur region is dry in summer and a bit more rainy in winter, allowing the cultivation of olive and other hard-leaf trees as well as beautiful flowering plants. Over the course of the year, though, the so-called "Mediterranean climate" is rather dry, and winters in the Côte d'Azur are relatively warm for its latitude (around the same as far northern Japan), since the cold north winds are blocked by the Alps. It seems natural to consider the area, with its own special climatic conditions, as a distinct region, but before the time of Lord Bloome the idea of the Côte d'Azur—the strip running from Toulon to Menton—was not yet a generally recognized concept. The area was simply a part of the Mediterranean coast, the southern frontier, dotted with a few insignificant fishing and mountain villages.

In 1832 cholera was spreading throughout Europe, and by 1834 it had broken out in America. At the time, the spread of the disease across the ocean was generally blamed on the increased number of transatlantic travelers. Whether or not that's true, the popularization of travel was certainly an unstoppable trend, and in 1835 the railroad first opened in Germany. Throughout Europe in the early nineteenth century horse-drawn carriages were being replaced by steam engines, and the number of travelers steadily increased.

On route from England to Nice, Lord Bloome stopped off in Cannes. It was then a mere fishing village of several thousand people, and Lord Bloome found it so charming that he built a summer house there. For 34 years, until his death at the age of 90, Lord Bloome spent every summer in Cannes, and every winter, when heavy fog covered the streets of London, he would tell his sceptical friends about it. Gradually, increasing numbers of British aristocrats began visiting Cannes and Nice, and finally Queen Victoria herself made the trip, all thanks to Lord Bloome and his affectionate publicity campaign for the region.

Until 1848, when the rail corridor opened between Marseilles and Avignon, it was difficult to reach the coast even from nearby parts of France. Rail lines were few in number, with 16 small companies sharing a total of 1,800–1,900 kilometers of routes. In the second half of the century, though, many of the small companies consolidated their routes and operations, and there was phenomenal growth.

Pierre Guiral is a professor at Provence University, the head of the Provence Historical Society, a recognized authority on nineteenth-century French society, and the author of the heavily researched book *Everyday Life in France during the Golden Age of Capitalism (1853–1879)*. According to Professor Guiral's book, railroads in France began connecting with lines in neighboring countries around 1857, during the Second Empire, and by 1870 six large railroad companies managed a total of 18,000 kilometers of railway routes throughout the country. That year saw the end of the empire and the beginning of the Third Republic, and France began a major modernization project, the Freycinet Plan. Although the social benefits would not be immediately apparent, the plan called for the modernization of the nation's harbors and the extension of rail routes to remote areas. The plan was completed in 1878–79 and it resulted in centralization of government control and the rapid development of industry. With the extension of the railway system came the revolutionary idea of rapid travel to distant places. One unexpected result was a phenomenal increase in agriculture; there was also a revival in religious pilgrimages. The capital-intensive tourism industry also made tremendous advances, while some doctors and other members of the bourgeoisie reportedly became rich by investing in hotels in newly developed hot spring resorts, though according to writer from Alfred Assolant, the most unusual result in France was the existence of Frenchmen who had actually traveled somewhere.

On the subject of the French summer "vacance," the traditional yearly paid holiday became standard in 1936, when Léon Blum's left-wing popular-front government concluded the Matignon Agreement between the French Employers' Federation and the nation's labor unions, and it was established as law. Today some 80% of Frenchmen travel by car outside the country during their vacation. And the Côte d'Azur, as in days of old, is still an international gathering spot where a cacophony of languages from around the world can be heard on its beaches.

CLASSIC HOTELS OF THE WORLD: VOL.3
CÔTE D'AZUR

Photography & Text:
Hiro Kishikawa

Supervision:
Jiro Hirashima

Art Direction:
Tsuneo Arima

Translation:
Robb Satterwhite

KAWADE SHOBO SHINSHA, Publishers, Tokyo.
2-32-2, Sendagaya, Shibuya-ku, Tokyo 151, Japan

Copyright © Kawade Shobo Shinsha Publishers Ltd. 1994
Photography and Text copyright © Hiro Kishikawa 1994

Printed in Japan by DAINIPPON PRINTING CO., LTD.

ISBN4-309-71593-1

CONTENTS

Hotel Negresco

37, Promenade des Anglais, BP 379, 06007 Nice Cedex, France

その特異なたたずまいから、今やニースの顔といわれるホテルである。20世紀の初め頃に、パリのレストランで最高のメートル・ドテル（給仕頭）と評価され、その後ニース市のカジノ・レストランを任されていたヘンリ・ネグレスコは、ニースのビーチに美しい宮殿様式によるホテル建設を切望していた。やがて彼は、企業家アレグザンドル・ダラックの資金協力を得て、ホテル・ネグレスコを1913年開業させた。設計は建築家エドゥアール・ニエルマン。しかし開業の１年後、第１次世界大戦が勃発。ホテルは戦傷者の病院として使われた。

1957年、現在のオーナー＝オージー夫妻がホテルを買収。夫人により全室が異なるクラシック・デザインでコーディネートされた。またホテル内部を飾る膨大なアンティークと歴史から、1974年には国の歴史的建造物の指定を受ける。ニースのビーチを彩る別名〝アンティーク博物館〟とも呼ばれる異色のホテルである。

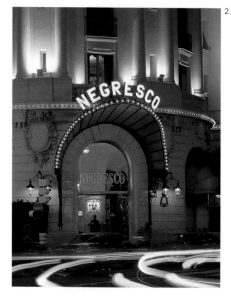

This odd-looking hotel is nicknamed "the face of Nice." Its founder was Henri Negresco, a well-known maître d'hôtel in Paris who later ran a casino restaurant in Nice. From the start of the twentieth century, Negresco's ambition was to construct a palace-style hotel on the beach, and in 1913, with financial backing from businessman Alexandre Darracq, he finally opened his hotel. Architect Edouard Niermans was the designer. One year after the opening, though, saw the start of World War I, and the hotel was converted to use as a hospital for war injuries.

Mr. and Mrs. Augier, the current owners, bought the hotel in 1957 and renovated it, with Mrs. Augier responsible for the classic interior design of the rooms. The hotel is now a showplace for beautiful antique furnishings, and in 1974 it was designated a National Historic Monument. This unusual beachfront Nice hotel is also known by another nickname, the "Antique Museum."

1，2: 宮殿様式や様々な建築様式を取り入れて建てられたホテル。第１次世界大戦後、ホテルはベルギーのホテル経営会社に買収された。3: ホテルの中央に設けられた「サロン・ロワイヤル」。楕円形ガラス・ドーム天井をもつニースで最も美しい宴会場。梁の化粧漆喰塗り彫刻とイオニア式柱頭部を24金の金箔で装飾。ここはフランスの歴史的建造物に指定されている（参照P-18～P-20）。

1, 2: This palatial-style hotel incorporates various architectural styles. A Belgian hotel management company bought the hotel at the end of World War I. 3: The centrally located *Salon Royal*, with its oval glass-domed ceiling, is said to be the most beautiful banquet facility in Nice. The stucco carvings and Ionic columns are covered in 24-carat gold leaf. It has been designated a National Historic Monument by the French government (See pages 18–20).

4

5

6

7

8

10

9

11

12

4: ドアマン。5: ベルマン。6: コンシェルジュ。ドア
マン、ベルマン、コンシェルジュのユニフォームは、
18世紀にフランスで使われたユニフォーム・デザイ
ン。7: 円形ドームを取り入れた「エントランス・ホー
ル」中央に置かれたベリー公爵（ルイ14世の王子）
の上半身像。右側にレセプション（写真:10）、左側
にコンシェルジュ・デスク（写真:6）が設けられてい
る。8: 長年総支配人を務めるミッシェル・パーマ
ー。9, 11:「エントランス・ホール」と「サロン・ロワイ
ヤル」の通路に設けられた階段。19世紀フランス
製飾り枠付き掛時計（カルテル）、ルイ15世の肖像
画などで飾られている。12: ホテル開業時のポスト
カード（ポストカード提供:ホテル・ネグレスコ）。

4: A doorman. 5: Bellmen. 6: Concierge.
The uniforms of the doormen, bellmen and concierges are based on eighteenth-century
French uniforms. 7: A bust of Duke Charles de
Berry, the grandson of Louis XIV, stands in the
center of the *Entrance Hall*. The reception desk
is on the right (see photo no. 10), the concierge
desk is on the left (see photo no. 6), and a dome
ceiling is overhead. 8: General Manager Michel
Palmer. 9, 11: A staircase leads from the pas-
sage between the *Entrance Hall* and the *Salon
Royal*. A nineteenth-century French cartel clock
(wall clock) stands on a tall pedestal, and a portrait of Louis XV hangs from the wall. 12: A postcard dating back to the hotel's opening (postcard courtesy of Hotel Negresco).

13

14

15

16

13-17：「エントランス・ホール」の隣に位置する「サロン・ルイ14世」。ここは主にレセプションやパーティーに使われる施設。壁を飾るルイ14世の肖像画は、ルイ14世時代の肖像画家H・リゴー（1659〜1743年）が描いた絶品。両端のカンデラーブラは17世紀製。木製天井はイタリアの名家マンチーニの離宮サンピエール・ダルビニイ城で使われていた17世紀製。重量10.5トンの暖炉はオートフォール城（ルイ14世の警護長を務めたオートフォール公爵の離宮）から運ばれた。木製彫刻ドアはアンリ4世の母皇ジャンヌ・ダルブル（1528〜1572年）邸で使われていた。このサロンは、ホテルのオーナーでもあり、会長兼経営責任者のオージー夫人により購入されたアンティーク。彼女自身がこのサロンのコーディネートを担当した。

13-17: The *Salon Louis XIV*, next to the *Entrance Hall*, is used mainly for receptions and parties. The portrait of Louis XIV was the work of Hyacinthe Rigaud (1659–1743), a portrait painter from the era of Louis XIV. The candelabra on either side were made in the seventeenth century, as was the wooden ceiling, which was originally from the Château Saint-Pierre d'Albigny (a palace owned by the famous Mancini family). The ten-and-a-half-ton fireplace was transported from the Château de Hautefort, the palace of the Duke of Hautefort, who was head of Louis XIV's royal guard. The carved wooden doors were from the mansion of Jeanne d'Albert (1528–1572), the mother of Henry IV. Mrs. Jeanne Augier, the hotel's owner, chairman and managing director, personally decorated the interior of this salon and purchased the antiques that furnish it.

18

18-22: ホテル開業時の内装デザインを残すメゾネット形式の「バー・ル・リレー」。木彫パネルで装飾されたイギリス・スタイルのバーである。壁を飾るタペストリーは1683年にベルギーで織られたテニールス様式。絨毯はナポレオン1世が寝室用に選んだパターンを再現したもの。柱と壁の突き出し燭台は19世紀製。これはフォンテーンブロー城のボールームで使われていたデザインの複製品。23: メリーゴーランドの雰囲気を取り入れた遊び心をもつ

レストラン「ラ・ロトンド」。宿泊者の朝食用レストランとして使われる。

18-22: The maisonette-style *Bar Le Relais*, a typical English-style bar with carved wood paneling, has retained its original interior. The tapestry on the wall was woven in Belgium in 1683 in the Teniers style, and the carpet is a reproduction of a pattern originally used in the bedroom of Emperor Napoléon I. The sconces

on the walls and columns were made in the nineteenth century. They are reproductions of the sconces in the Ballroom at the Château de Fontainebleau. 23: *La Rotonde* has a merry-go-round motif and a relaxed, playful atmosphere. It serves as a breakfast restaurant for hotel guests.

19

20

21

22

23

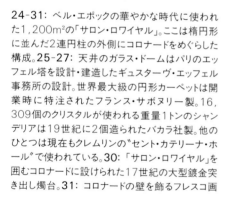

24

25

24-31: ベル・エポックの華やかな時代に使われた1,200m²の「サロン・ロワイヤル」。ここは楕円形に並んだ2連円柱の外側にコロナードをめぐらした構成。25-27: 天井のガラス・ドームはパリのエッフェル塔を設計・建造したギュスターヴ・エッフェル事務所の設計。世界最大級の円形カーペットは開業時に特注されたフランス・サボヌリー製。16,309個のクリスタルが使われる重量1トンのシャンデリアは19世紀に2個造られたバカラ社製。他のひとつは現在もクレムリンの〝セント・カテリーナ・ホール″で使われている。30:「サロン・ロワイヤル」を囲むコロナードに設けられた17世紀の大型鍍金突き出し燭台。31: コロナードの壁を飾るフレスコ画のひとつは1912年にアーティストのルュカにより描かれた。

24-31: The 1,200-square-meter (12,917-square-foot) *Salon Royal* dates back to the glamorous Belle Epoque era. Around the room is a double row of columns forming an elliptical colonnade. 25-27: The glass dome ceiling was created by the workshop of Alexandre Gustave Eiffel, the engineer who designed and built the Eiffel Tower. The magnificent round carpet was specially ordered from the Savonnerie factory and installed when the hotel opened. The one-ton chandelier, with 16,309 individual crystals, was made in the nineteenth century by the Baccarat Company. The chandelier is actually one of a pair made at the same time; its mate is now in the "Hall of St. Catherine" in the Kremlin in Russia. 30: Seventeenth-century large-size wall sconces illuminate the colonnade area surrounding the *Salon Royal*. 31: One of the fresco paintings on the colonnade area walls was painted in 1912 by an artist named Lucas.

26

27

28

29

30

31

32
33 34

32-34: アンピール様式でコーディネートされた集宴会場「サロン・マセナ」。1797年、チューリッヒやリヴォリでの戦いを勝利に導きナポレオンに「勝利の女神の愛児」と称され、隣接地に別邸を所有していたアンドレ・マセナ元帥（1758〜1817年）から命名されている。**32：**ルイ14世の幼年期の肖像画が飾られている。

32–34: *Salon Masséna* is a meeting and banquet area decorated in Empire style. It is named after André Masséna, Duke of Rivoli (1758–1817), the French marshal under Napoléon I. Masséna was called the "Beloved Child of the Goddess of Victory" because of the battles he won at Rivoli and Zürich. He owned a villa next to the site of the hotel. **32:** A childhood portrait of Louis XIV hangs from the wall.

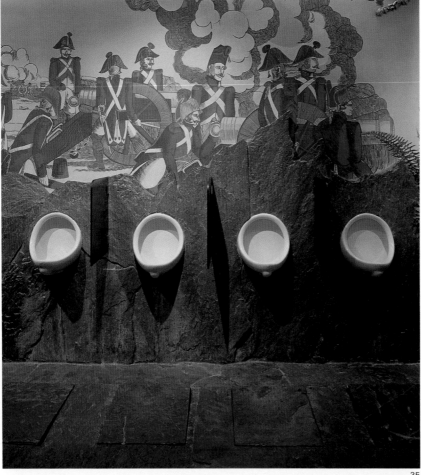

35

36

37

38

35-38: ホテル1階に1967年につくられたパブリック・トイレット。男性用手洗室は19世紀初期に戦場で使われた野営陣地のテント・デザインを取り入れコーディネート。最初の利用者はカンボジア国王シアヌーク殿下だった。35: 男性小用手洗室は体重で水が流れる電動式（正方形の立ち位置がスイッチ）。36: 移動式洗面台、壁ライトに利用した鉄兜は19世紀のアンティーク。37: 18世紀の女性用衣装を窓内部に展示した女性用手洗室。38: 入口のトイレット係。使用後は心付けが必要。39, 40: 階段1階に置かれた19世紀フランス製カルテル時計と2階のパブリック・スペースを飾る18世紀製アルムワール（衣装箪笥）。41, 42: 「エントランス・ホール」のボヘミアン・クリスタル・シャンデリアと壁ライト。

35-38: Public toilets were installed on the ground floor in 1967. The design of the men's room is inspired by early nineteenth-century army camp tents. The first person to use the facilities was King Sihanouk of Cambodia. 35: Standing in front of one of the urinals in the men's room activates a switch in the floor and causes water to flow in the urinal. 36: The movable washbasins and the steel helmets used in the wall lights are nineteenth-century antiques. 37: Eighteenth-century women's clothing fills the window of the ladies' room. 38: An attendant stands at the bathroom entrance; patrons generally leave a tip after using the facilities. 39, 40: A nineteenth-century French cartel clock occupies the ground-floor stairway landing, and an eighteenth-century armoire (clothes closet) stands in the public space on the first floor. 41, 42: The *Entrance Hall* is lit by a Bohemian crystal chandelier and wall lights.

39

40

41

42

43

44

45 46

43-48: ミシュラン二つ星（1993年度）の「シャンテクレール」レストラン。43，44: レストランに接続するプライヴェート・ダイニング・ルーム「サロン・レジァンス」。12枚のマリーヌ（ベルギー中北部の都市）製レザー・パネル、ルイ15世様式鍍金木彫鏡、リージェンシー様式コモードなどが使われている。45，46: リージェンシー様式で装飾された「シャンテクレール」レストランのダイニング・ルーム。木彫パネルはリヨン北部の町マコン近郊にあるシャートル城のステイト・ルームから運ばれた1751年製のアンティーク。カーペットは18世紀から使われているオーピュッソン・カーペットのデザイン・モチーフを取り入れ、クラシックなサボヌリー様式で織られたもの。

43-48: The Michelin two-star (1993 edition) restaurant *Chantecler*. 43, 44: The *Salon Régence* private dining room is connected to the restaurant. The interior includes twelve leather panels made in Maline (a town in north-central Belgium), a Louis XV gilt wood mirror, and Regency commodes. 45, 46: The dining room at *Chantecler* is decorated in Regency style. The antique wood panels were made in 1751 and were originally used in the state room at the Château de Chaintre in the village of Mâcon to the north of Lyon. The classic Savonnerie-style carpet incorporates design motifs used in Aubusson carpets since the eighteenth century.

47

48

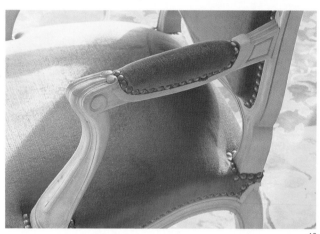

49

50

51

52

53

54

55

56

57

58

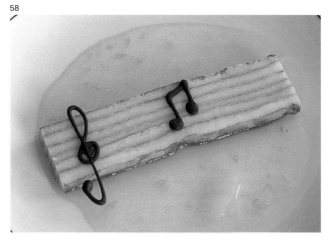

47: 食器はベルナルドのリモージュ焼が使われる。48:「シャンテクレール」レストランのスタッフ。49: 赤いヴェルヴェット布地張りの椅子はルイ15世様式フォートイユ（肘掛け椅子）。50: ホテルのロゴ・マークが入ったクリスタル・グラス。51: 木彫パネル壁に飾られる肖像画はルイ14世の王女オルレアン公爵夫人。52: 左が総料理長のドミニク・ルストン。1958年ストラスブール生まれ。ミシュラン三つ星のレストラン「オーベルジュ・ド・リル」と「ミヨネ」で修行、1989年から現職。右がレストラン・マネージャーのA・ハルマ。53: ランゴスチーヌのサラダ。54: イトヨリのフィレ、アーティチョーク添え。55: 平目の網焼き、オイスターのペルシーヤード。56: 鹿肉のフィレ、クールジェット添え。57: カシス・ジュース漬け梨の冷菓。58: ローカル芳香入り音符型シャーベット。

47: The servingware used here is Limoges china by Bernardaud. 48: The restaurant staff at *Chantecler*. 49: The Louis XV *fauteuils* (upholstered armchairs) are covered in red velvet. 50: Crystal glass etched with the hotel logo. 51: A portrait of the Duchess of Orleans, daughter of King Louis XV, hangs from the wood-paneled walls. 52: At left is Chef de Cuisine Dominique Le Stanc, born in Strausbourg in 1958. Chef Le Stanc trained at the Michelin three-star restaurant *Auberge de l'Ill* and at *Mionnay*, and began working here in 1989. At right is restaurant manager Alain Harma. 53: Prawn salad with fennel and pepper confits (*salade de langoustines au fenouil et poivrons confits*). 54: Fillets of mullet with artichokes (*filets de rougets en salade d'artichauts du Pays*). 55: Grilled turbot, oysters with garlic and parsley, and creamed leeks (*turbot grillé, jus de volaille, huîtres en persillade, poireaux à la crème*). 56: Fillet of venison with olives, dried tomatoes and zucchini risotto (*filet de chevreuil aux olives, tomates séchées, risotto de courgettes*). 57: Pear poached in blackcurrant juice, with verbena and blackcurrant ice (*glace de verveine et cassis, poires pochées au jus de cassis*). 58: Sherbets with flavors of the countryside (*partition de sorbets aux parfums de l'Arrière-Pays*).

59

60

61

62

63

64

65

59-65: ニースのビーチを180度眺望する半楕円形バルコニーを付設した「スイート(321/322号室)」。応接間、寝室、浴室で構成される。**59, 63:** 朝食のルーム・サービスはゲストの好みにより応接間、寝室、バルコニーを選ぶことができる。**60, 61:** 応接間で使われるルイ15世様式マルケトリー・キャビネットとナポレオン3世マルケトリー・センター・テーブル。**62:** ハウスキーパーのスーパーバイザー。**63, 65:** 寝室で撮影したハウスキーパーとナイト・テーブルのテーブル・ランプ。ホテルの各階段スペースはフランス特有の様式(6階はナポレオン3世様式、5階はアンピール様式、4階はルイ15世様式、3階はモダン様式)で装飾され、アンティークの家具、タペストリー、絵画などが飾られている。

59-65: *Suite 321/322* includes a semi-elliptical balcony with a panoramic 180-degree view of Nice's beach. The suite includes a sitting room, bedroom and bathroom. **59, 63:** Room service will serve breakfast either in the bedroom, in the sitting room, or on the balcony, according to guests' wishes. **60, 61:** A Louis XV marquetry cabinet and Napoléon III marquetry center table furnish the sitting room. **62:** A housekeeping supervisor. **63, 65:** A housekeeper, shown in the bedroom, and a table lamp on the night table. The stairway landings on each floor represent different French design periods. The antique furniture, tapestries and paintings are all Napoléon III style pieces on the fifth floor, Empire style on the fourth floor, Louis XV style on the third floor, and modern style on the second floor.

66

67

68

69

70

71

72

66, 67: 羊の頭部彫刻をアームヘッドに付けたベルジェール（クッション付き安楽椅子）が使われている「スイート（220/221号室）」の応接間。応接間の壁ライトは突き出し燭台を再利用したアンティーク。68: ビーチ側に設けられた「スイート（215/216号室）」の応接間。寝室の天井はフランス国旗の3色でコーディネートされている。69: コロナ・ベッドを設けた「スイート（121/122号室）」の寝室。70, 71: アンティークのナポレオン3世家具でコーディネートされた「209号室」。ベッドは（当時の金額で1台約1,800万円）オークションで落札された。ブル・エンクアンアール（象眼コーナー家具）はべっ甲の表面に真鍮の葉飾りを象眼した貴重品。

72-74: 四柱天蓋ベッドを設けた「419号室」。壁ライトは草花をデザインした珍しいもの。

66, 67: The sitting room of *Suite 220/221* includes an unusual *bergère* (cushioned armchair) featuring carved ram's heads on the armheads. The sitting room wall lights are antique sconces. 68: The sitting room of *Suite 215/216*, which faces the beach. The bedroom ceiling is painted in the colors of the French flag. 69: The bedroom of *Suite 121/122* has a corona bed. 70, 71: *Room 209* is filled with antique Napoléon III furniture. The bed was purchased at auction for 300,000 French francs (US$50,000). It is a

beautiful example of *boulle encoignure* (furniture with inlaid corners), with inlaid cut-brass foliage on a tortoise-shell surface. 72–74: *Room 419* has a four-poster canopied bed and unusual wall lights with a flowering plant design.

73

74

75

75-88: フランス・アンピール様式でコーディネートされた「スイート・アンペリアル（1804号室）」。皇帝ナポレオン1世（在位1804〜1815年/1769〜1821年）の即位年を記した名称が使われている。75, 84: 寝室のデザイン・コーディネーションは、1810年に再改装されたマルメゾン城（一時、ナポレオンの居城として使われ現在は国立博物館）の〝ジョセフィーヌ皇后の寝室〟をデザインしたジャコブ・デマルテル（1739〜1814年/家具製造者。ルイ16世様式、アンピール様式の代表者）のデザインを模したものと思われる。78: 2カ所のシッティング・エリアとアンピール様式の寝室を設けたL字形の寝室兼応接間、浴室、副寝室から構成され、天井には空が描かれている。

75-88: The *Suite Impériale (Room 1804)* is decorated in French Empire style. The room number commemorates the year when Emperor Napoléon I (1769-1821; reigned 1804-1815) ascended the throne. 75, 84: The interior of the bedroom is believed to be a reproduction of a design by Jacob Desmalter, who decorated the bedroom of the Empress Josephine at the Château Malmaison when it was remodeled in 1810. The chateau served temporarily as Napoléon's palace; it is now a national museum. Jacob Desmalter (1739-1814) was a furniture maker and an influential designer in the Louis XIV and French Empire styles. 78: The suite contains an L-shaped combination bedroom/sitting room with two sitting areas and an Empire-style bedroom area; there is also a bathroom and a guest bedroom. The ceiling is painted to resemble the sky.

76

77

79

80

81

82

83

84

85

86

87

80, 88: アンピール様式のサイド・キャビネットは1810年代製作のアンティークと思われる。上部の肖像画はナポレオン1世。81, 82: バス・アメニティとバス・タオル。シンクとバスタブは黄金色で統一。83: 入口のドア枠装飾は木製イオニア柱とトライアングラー・ペディメントで構成。85-87: アンピール様式のカップボードとディティール。フランス・アンピール様式（1801～1815年）の家具は、ナポレオンのエジプト遠征にも参加した外交官・画家でもあったドノン（1747～1825年）が出版した出版物『上エジプト遺跡旅行記』を参考に、彼の委嘱でジャコブ・デマルテルが製作した。ドノンはナポレオン1世時代、全国美術館の総館長を務めた人物。1808年、彼の出版物はドイツ、イタリー、英国で出版され家具メーカーに大きな影響を与えた。

80, 88: The Empire-style side cabinet is an antique believed to date back to the 1810s. The portrait above is of Napoléon I. 81, 82: Bathroom amenities and bath towels. The sink and bathtub are both gold in color. 83: The entrance door frame is made up of wooden Ionic columns and a triangular pediment. 85–87: An Empire-style cupboard, and furniture details. The French Empire furniture (1801–1815) was crafted by Jacob Desmalter and commissioned by Baron Denon. Denon (1747–1825) was a statesman and painter who took part in Napoléon's expedition to Egypt. He was also in charge of France's art museums during the reign of Napoléon. Denon's book about the expedition, *Voyage dans la Basse et Haute Egypte*, appeared in 1808 in Germany, Italy and England and had a tremendous influence on furniture makers in those countries. Desmalter based many of the details of his furniture design on illustrations from the book.

88

89: 年間平均気温15度という快適な環境に恵まれたニースの夕暮れ。19世紀末にイギリス人の富裕階級で賑わったことから、ビーチに伸びる歩道をプロムナード・デザングレ(イギリス人の散歩道)と呼ぶ。当時の平均気温が現在よりも数度低かったこと、さらにこの時代ニースまでの鉄道網が完備されたことが幸いした。欧州の貴族や産業革命を終え富を手中にしていたイギリス人たちがここに集い、避寒のための冬季リゾートとしてコート・ダジュールは最も華やかな時代を20世紀初頭に迎えたという。しかし、ホテル・ネグレスコの創設者H・ネグレスコは開業の1年後に勃発した第1次世界大戦により破産、失意のうちにパリで52歳の生涯を閉じたという。コート・ダジュールとはカシスからマントンに至る海岸地帯を指し、ここが1860年にイタリアからフランス領となったことから、イタリア文化圏の影響を

現在も色濃く残す地域である。90: ホテル開業の前年(1912年)、V・ロランにより描かれたホテル・ポスター(ポスター提供:ホテル・ネグレスコ)。91: 20世紀初頭に撮影されたプロムナード・デザングレのポストカード。

89: Evening in Nice, an area blessed with a pleasant climate and an average year-round temperature of 15℃ (59°F). The beachfront walkway is called the Promenade des Anglais (Promenade of the English), after the affluent English who gathered there at the end of the nineteenth century. In those days the average temperature was several degrees cooler, and the train network had been recently completed to extend as far as Nice, so wealthy English as well as European aristocrats and industrialists

gathered here. The early years of the twentieth century corresponded with the Côte d'Azur's most elegant era as a winter resort. The year after the opening of the Hotel Negresco, however, saw the outbreak of World War I, and hotel founder Henri Negresco soon went bankrupt. He died in Paris, penniless and heartbroken, at the age of 52. Looking at the Côte d'Azur today, one can still feel the strong influence of Italian culture. The beachfront area stretching from Cassis to Menton was transferred from Italian to French jurisdiction in 1860, but the area has retained much of its Italian personality to this day. 90: A poster created by artist V. Lorant in 1912, the year before the hotel opened (poster courtesy of Hotel Negresco). 91: A postcard of the Promenade des Anglais dating from the early twentieth century.

89

90

91

154. - NICE. - Promenade des Anglais

Hotel Westminster Concorde

27, Promenade des Anglais, 06000 Nice, France

ニースに現存する最も古いグランド・ホテルのひとつ。最初の名称はホテル・ウエストミンスター。開業は1880年。創業者はグリンダ家。ビーチに延びる名高いデザングレ道路（イギリス人の散歩道）沿いの一等地に建設された。1904年に行なわれた増設工事の際、フレスコ画天井で飾られたグランド・ホールと荘厳な2カ所のサロンがつくられた。そのうちのひとつのサロンには生演奏用の天井桟敷が付設され、当時ここでディナー・ダンスが毎晩繰りひろげられたという。1961年、創業者の子孫にあたるドクター・J・P・グリンダ氏がホテルを相続。近代設備を導入するリノヴェーションが行なわれたが、2カ所の貴重なサロンはそのまま残された。

19世紀末に建てられたコート・ダジュールの多くのグランド・ホテルは、壊されたりアパートメントに転用されたりした。しかし、ここはニースの華やかだったベル・エポックの喧噪を伝える数少ない貴重なホテルとなっている。

This is one of Nice's oldest Grand Hotels, first opening in 1880 on the famous beachfront "Promenade des Anglais." It was originally founded by the Grinda family as the Hotel Westminster. In 1904 the hotel was renovated and enlarged; at that time two magnificent salons and a Grand Hall with a ceiling fresco were added. One of the salons included a viewing gallery for watching live performances, and the salons were also the scene of nightly dinner dances. In 1961 the hotel was inherited by Docter J.P. Grinda, a descendant of the founders. He carried out extensive renovation work, adding modern facilities and carefully restoring the two historic salons.

Of the many grand hotels built along the Côte d'Azur at the end of the nineteenth century, most have been either demolished or converted to apartments. This is one of the few survivors dating back to Nice's lively Belle Epoque, standing as a living reminder of those glamorous days.

1, 2: 6階建、150室を設けたホテル。現在の外装は、1904年の増設でつくられたデザイン。1960年代までは、ビーチ・サイドのすべての窓に観音開きのシャッターが付設され、リゾート地に相応しい純白のファサードで統一されていた。3: 最大の宴会場「サロン・プレジダン」。化粧漆喰塗り彫刻の天井と壁、4個の大シャンデリアで飾られている（P-54, 55参照）。

1, 2: This six-story hotel has 150 guest rooms. The present exterior dates back to the 1904 renovation. Until the 1960s all the rooms on the beach side had folding shutters, and the entire façade was painted a dazzling shade of white. 3: The *Salon Président* is the largest banquet room, with stucco walls and ceiling and four large chandeliers (see pages 54 and 55).

4: 19世紀末に撮影されたニースのビーチ。左側中央の建物がホテル・ウエストミンスター。この時代埠頭にドーム型のカジノがつくられ、有産階級の避寒地として賑わっていた（写真提供：ホテル・ウエストミンスター・コンコルド）。5: レストラン「ラ・ファルニエンテ」に飾られる19世紀末期のニースの油絵。6: ルイ14世とマセナ元帥の肖像レリーフが両壁に付けられている風除室。7: 中国家具でコーディネートされた「サロン・シノワ」。8: 20世紀初頭のホテル。奥がカジノ（写真提供：ホテル・ウエストミンスター・コンコルド）。9: ニースの歴史的な絵画コレクションで飾られる「エントランス・ホール」。これらの絵画は総支配人ピエール・グイラン夫人ジゼルにより20年をかけ集められた。10: ホテル1階の平面図。

4: The beach at Nice at the end of the nineteenth century. The building to the left of center is the Hotel Westminster. During this period a domed casino stood on the wharf, and the area was a popular winter resort for wealthy vacationers from throughout Europe (photo courtesy of Hotel Westminster Concorde). 5: An oil painting of Nice in the late nineteenth century hangs in *Le Farniente* restaurant. 6: A vestibule, with reliefs of Louis XIV and Duke Masséna carving on the walls. 7: Chinese furniture fills the *Salon Chinois*. 8: The hotel at the beginning of the twentieth century. The casino is at the rear (photo courtesy of Hotel Westminster Concorde). 9: The *Entrance Hall* contains a collection of historic paintings of Nice. The collection was assembled over the course of twenty years by Mme. Giséle Gouirand, the wife of General Manager Pierre Gouirand. 10: A floor plan of the hotel's ground floor.

9

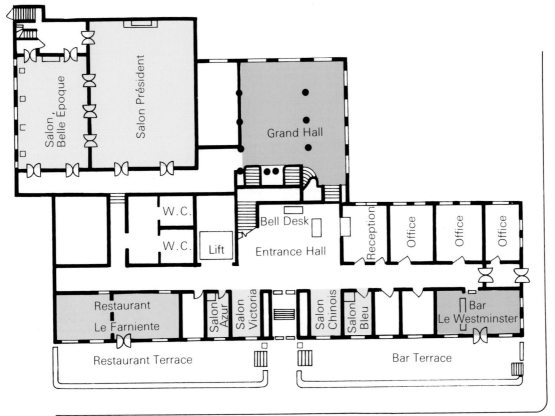

10

Promenade des Anglais

15

14

11, 12:「エントランス・ホール」に設けられた階段室。以前、ここにエレヴェーターが設置されていた。13-19: フレスコ画天井と3本の円柱で飾られた「グランド・ホール」。ここはクロイスター（修道院の方形の中庭を囲む列柱廊）の一部を模したデザインで構成され、階段室から直接「グランド・ホール」につながる設計が取り入れられている。天井のフレスコ画は楽器を演奏するケンタウロス（腰から上が人間の姿をした馬身の怪物）が描かれた珍しいもの。中央に置かれたソファーはその形からロトンドと呼ばれる。この「グランド・ホール」はレセプションやお茶を楽しむラウンジとしても使われる。

11, 12: The stairway leading from the *Entrance Hall*. Once there was an elevator here. 13-19: Adorning the ceiling of the *Grand Hall* is an unusual fresco painting of centaurs (mythical creatures that are half man and half horse) playing musical instruments. A number of columns support the ceiling; the design is based on that of a colonnade surrounding the central courtyard at a cloistered monastery. The shape of the sofa at the center of the room has given it the name "Rotonde." The *Grand Hall* is used for receptions and as a tea lounge, and it connects directly to the main stairway.

16

17

18

19

20

16-19:「グランド・ホール」で使われるクラシックな家具。16: 背もたれ上部にスワンズ・ネックと松かさをデザインした珍しいアームチェアー。ヴィクトリア時代に英国で作られたものと思われる。17: ルイ15世様式フォートイユ（肘掛け椅子）とルイ15世様式カナペ（ソファー）。18: U字型背もたれのアームチェアー。これはリージェンシー様式のデザインが一部取り入れられている。19: ディスプレイ・キャビネット。イタリアで製作されたアンティークと思われる。20-22: バー「ル・ウエストミンスター」。昼食時には軽食も提供し、テラスを付設する。

16-19: Classic furnishings in the *Grand Hall*. 16: The back of this armchair features an unusual swan's neck and pine cone design. It is believed to date back to Victorian-era England. 17: A *fauteuil* (armchair) and *canapé* (sofa) in Louis XV style. 18: A Regency armchair with U-shaped back. 19: This antique display cabinet is believed to be Italian. 20-22: Bar *Le Westminster* includes a terrace; it serves light meals at lunchtime.

21

22

23

24

25

26

27

28

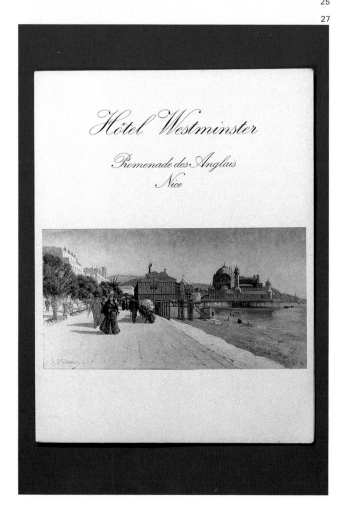

29

23-29: テラス・エリアを付設したレストラン「ル・フェルニェンテ（無為）」。元来この名称はイタリア語で〝何もしないこと〟を意味し、リゾートならではの命名。レストランの内装はクリーム色を基調としたカラー・スキーム。籐細工の背もたれ、脚部にX型の張り材を使った椅子はルイ15世様式シェーズ（サイド・チェアー）と呼ばれるもの。23-26: 食器は絵付け模様が熱で変色しないデコール・イナルテラブル。この食器の絵柄は〝インドの花々〟と名付けられたラファルジのリモージュ焼。ナイフはクリストフルが使われる。27: メニュー・カバーは19世紀末のニースを描いた絵が使われる。28: マネージャーとウエイトレス。

23-29: *Le Farniente* restaurant, in the terrace area, is decorated in a cream color scheme. The name means 'the idler' in Italian, an appropriate name for a resort-area establishment. The Louis XV chaise side chairs have canework backs and X-shaped leg stretchers. 23-26: The Limoges tableware is heat-resistant *décor inaltérable*. The pattern is called "Fleurs des Indes," by Lafarge. Knives are by Cristofle. 27: The menu cover is a late nineteenth-century painting of Nice. 28: The restaurant manager and a waitress.

30

32

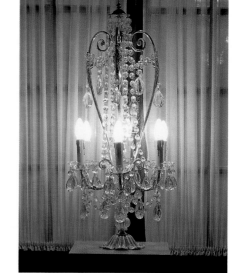

31

33

30-34: イタリア・ルネサンス様式の格天井と大シャンデリアを吊った「サロン・ベル・エポック」。7.77×14m、総床面積110m²。レセプション形式で150名、バンケット形式で70名を収容する。ここはゲストの朝食用レストランとして使われる。31: 3カ所のドア（カーテンの裏に設けられている）で隣の「サロン・プレジダン」とつながる設計が取り入れられ、素晴らしい漆喰装飾の壁で飾られている。33: 3カ所の窓側に設けられた台座つきの小型カンデラーブラ（枝付き燭台：元来はロウソクを使った照明）のひとつ。

30–34: *Salon Belle Epoque* has large chandeliers hanging from the Italian Renaissance–style coffered ceilings. The room is 7.8 by 14 meters (25.5 by 45.8 feet), with a total area of 110 square meters (1,184 square feet). It accommodates 150 persons for receptions and 70 for banquets, and it also serves as a breakfast restaurant for hotel guests. 31: Beautiful decorative plasterwork adorns the walls. Three doors (behind curtains) link this room to the adjacent *Salon Président*. 33: One of three small candelabra on pedestals, on the window side of the room.

35

36

37

38

39 40

35-40: 演奏用の桟敷を設けた最大の宴会場「サロン・プレジダン」。10×18.4m、総床面積184m²。レセプション形式で500名、バンケット形式で180名を収容する。写真40の右側カーテン背後が「サロン・ベル・エポック」につながる。ここは化粧漆喰塗り彫刻の壁と天井、4個の真鍮製シャンデリアで飾られている。「サロン・プレジダン」と「サロン・ベル・エポック」はニースが最も華やかな時代だったベル・エポック（1890〜1914年頃）の後期にディナー・ダンス用の会場として毎晩使われ、活況を呈したという。

35-40: *Salon Président* is the largest banquet area, with galleries for viewing live musical performances. The room measures 10 by 18.4 meters (32.8 by 60.3 feet), with a total area of 184 square meters (1,978 square feet), and it can accommodate up to 500 persons for receptions and 180 for banquets. The room here has decorative plasterwork on the walls and ceiling as well as four brass chandeliers. *Salon Belle Epoque* can be reached through the back of the garden at the right side of photo no. 40. During the later years of the "Belle Epoque" (1890–1914), when social activities in Nice were reaching their height, the nightly dinner dances in the *Salon Président* and *Salon Belle Epoque* were an important part of that scene.

41

42

43

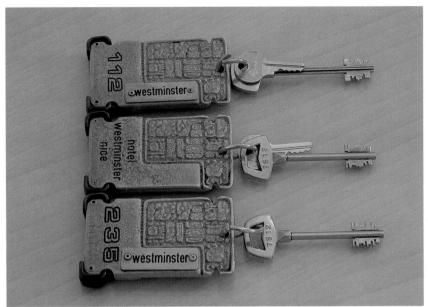
45

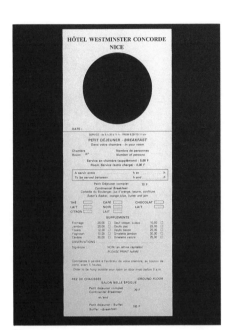
44

46

47

41-47: 開業時から使われる家具をそのまま保存した「235号室」。浴室は現代設備を導入しリノヴェーションされている。43: ルイ15世様式紫檀製・オルモル合金飾り・弓型表面アルムワール・ア・グラス（鏡付き衣装箪笥）は19世紀末期にフランスで製作され、パリで販売された数少ない貴重品。44: 朝食用ドアタッグ。45: 真鍮製の大型キー・ホルダーが使われる。46，47: ルイ15世様式紫檀製・オルモル合金飾り・マルケトリー・ライティング・テーブルと同じ様式のベッドも19世紀末期に製作されたものと思われる。このホテルは、ニースに現存する2番目に古いホテルである。

41–47: Antique furniture dating from the hotel's opening is still used in *Room 235*, although the bathroom has been renovated and outfitted with modern facilities. **43:** The Louis XV bow-fronted *armoire à glace*, a rare late-nineteenth-century French antique, is finished in kingwood and gilded with ormolu. **44:** A breakfast door tag. **45:** A large brass key holder. **46, 47:** This Louis XV ormolu-gilded kingwood marquetry writing table and matching bed are also believed to date back to the late nineteenth century. This is the second-oldest hotel in Nice.

Hotel Martinez

73, La Croisette, 06406 Cannes Cedex, France

20世紀初めまでのコート・ダジュールは、王侯貴族と富裕階級にのみ開かれた避寒のリゾートだった。しかし第１次世界大戦を終えた頃には、年間を通じて人々が集うリゾートに発展・変貌していた。この時代、カンヌのビーチに新しいグランド・ホテルが建てられることになった。創業者は、パリやモナコでホテル・マネージャーを長年務めたシシリー生まれのエマニュエル・マルティネズ。ホテルは、1927年12月に建設を開始し、1929年１月に開業。しかし開業時のホテルは、２階部分までしか完成していなかったという。8階建、変形U字型平面をもつホテルの設計はニースの建築家パレルモ。インテリア・デコレーションをロンドンの名店ワーリング・アンド・ギローが担当、アール・デコ様式でホテル内部が装飾された。

第２次世界大戦後、一時ホテルは政府の監督下におかれた。1982年にはコンコルド・ホテルズ・グループに買収され、リノヴェーションを終え今日に至っている。

Le " MARTINEZ "

Until the early twentieth century the Côte d'Azur was strictly a winter resort, popular with aristocrats and wealthy European vacationers. With the end of World War I, though, the area was transformed into a year-round resort. It was during this era that Sicilian-born Emanuel Martinez, a hotel manager with long years of experience in both Paris and Monaco, built his new "Grand Hotel" on the beach in Cannes. Construction began in December 1927 and the hotel opened in January 1929, although only two stories (the ground floor and first floor) were finished in time. A local Nice architect named Palermo designed the 8-story, U-shaped structure, and the famous London store of Waring and Gillow was responsible for the interiors, which were done in Art Deco style.

After World War II the local government took control temporarily, and in 1982 the Concorde Hotels Group bought the hotel and renovated it.

1：開業時に描かれたホテル・イラスト。この時代、屋外温水プールは完備していなかった（イラスト提供：ホテル・マルティネス）。2：ホテルの夜景。プールサイドには夏季のみ開店するレストラン「ル・グリル・デュ・マルティネス」が設けられる。3：天井を鏡張りにした「レセプション・ホール」。椅子、ソファー、テーブルはアール・デコ様式の複製品でコーディネートされている。

1: The hotel when it first opened; the outdoor warm-water pool was not yet complete (illustration courtesy of Hotel Martinez). 2: A nighttime view. *Le Grill du Martinez*, a poolside restaurant, is open in the summertime. 3. The *Reception Hall* has a mirrored ceiling; the chairs, sofas and tables are Art Deco reproductions.

4

5

4: 左がドアマン。右がベルマン。5: コンシェルジュ。6: 1950年に埠頭から撮影されたホテル(写真提供:ホテル・マルティネス)。7: ホテルの総支配人、パトリック・スィカー。シャトー・デスクリモン(ホテル)を経て、1985年にパリのホテル・ルテシアの総支配人に就任。1989年から現職。8: 専用埠頭から望むホテル。カンヌのホテルのなかで最大規模のプライヴェート・ビーチをもち、ここに4〜9月の間「ル・レストラン・ド・ラ・プラージュ(200席)」が設けられる。ホテルの建物背後には、7面のコートとスナック・バーを付設した「カンヌ・テニス・クラブ」がある。9: ホテル1階の平面図。ホテルはカンヌのビーチに並行して延びるクロワゼット大通りに面した好立地に建つ。

4: A doorman (left) and bellman (right). 5: A concierge. 6: A view of the hotel from a pier in 1950 (photo courtesy of Hotel Martinez). 7: General Manager Patrick Scicard started his career at the Château d'Esclimont (hotel), then became general manager of Hotel Lutétia in Paris in 1985. He has been here since 1989. 8: The hotel, seen from its pier. It boasts the largest private beach of any Cannes hotel, where the 200-seat *Restaurant de la Plage* operates from April through September each year. Behind the hotel is the *Cannes Tennis Club*, with seven courts and a snack bar. 9: A floor plan of the ground floor. The hotel occupies a prime site on the Boulevard de la Croisette, the major avenue running parallel to the Cannes beach.

6

7

8

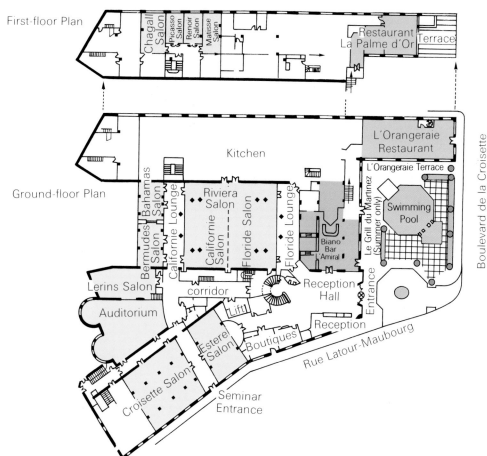

First-floor Plan

Chagall Salon
Picasso Salon
Renoir Salon
Matisse Salon

Restaurant
La Palme d'Or

Terrace

Ground-floor Plan

Kitchen

L'Orangeraie
Restaurant

L'Orangeraie Terrace

Boulevard de la Croisette

Bermudes Salon
Bahamas Salon
Californie Lounge

Riviera
Salon

Californie
Salon

Floride Salon

Floride Lounge

Piano
Bar
L'Amiral

Le Grill du Martinez
(Summer only)

Swimming
Pool

Lerins Salon

corridor

Reception
Hall

Entrance

Auditorium

Lift

Estérel Salon

Boutiques

Reception

Croisette Salon

Seminar
Entrance

Rue Latour-Maubourg

9

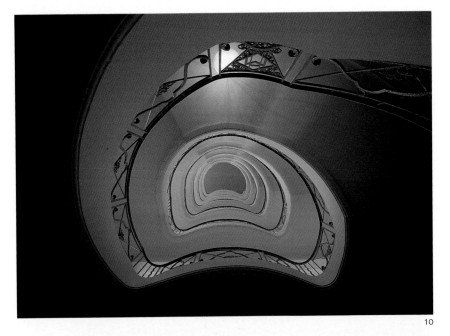

10

11

12

13

14

15

16

10-16: 開業時のデザインをそのまま残したクラシックな階段室。11, 12: 階段の親柱と手摺子は鉄製。手摺子にはホテルのロゴ・マークがデザインされている。13: 「レセプション・ホール」で使われるランタン形の天井照明。14, 16: 階段室の各フロアーには安楽椅子とテーブルを置いたスペースが設けられ、アール・デコの家具が飾られる。15: ホテル開業前後の写真。左上が1928年の造成工事の写真、右上と右下が現在のプール・エリアに設けられていたレストラン「ラ・テラス・アンソレイエ」、左下が最初の宴会場としてつくられた「ラ・サル・デ・フェート（祭りの大サロン）」（写真提供:ホテル・マルティネス）。

10–16: The original design of the staircase has been preserved. 11, 12: The central pillar and banisters are iron. The hotel logo is incorporated in the design of the banisters. 13: Lantern-shaped ceiling lights illuminate the *Reception Hall*. 14, 16: Art Deco furnishings occupy the staircase landings; the rest areas at each level are furnished with tables and easy chairs. 15: Some photographs from the time of the hotel's opening: construction work in 1928 (upper left); *La Terrasse Ensoleillée*, a restaurant in the area now occupied by the pool (upper right and lower right); and *La Salle des Fêtes*, the hotel's first banquet facility (lower left; photos courtesy of Hotel Martinez).

17

18

19

20

21

22

23

24

25

26

17-21,25: ゲストの朝食用レストランとして使われる「オランジュレ・レストラン」。200席。昼にライト・ランチョンが提供され、日曜日はオードヴル・ビュッフェも楽しめる。ヘルス・コンシャス（健康を意識した）のメニュー（600Kcal）も用意されている。銀製品はクリストフル、食器はアヴィランドのリモージュ焼。22: ホテル開業時のポスター（ポスター提供：ホテル・マルティネス）。23,24,26: カクテル・ラウンジの機能をもつピアノ・バー「アミラル（海軍総督）」。メゾネット形式を取り入れモダン・デザインにコーディネートされている。

17–21, 25: *L'Orangerie* Restaurant seats 200 serves breakfast to hotel guests. There is also a light luncheon on weekdays, an hors d'oeuvre buffet on Sundays, and a "health-conscious" menu that totals only 600 calories. Silverware is by Cristofle, and the Limoges china is by Haviland. 22: A poster from the hotel's opening (poster courtesy of Hotel Martinez). 23, 24, 26: The piano bar *L'Amiral* ('The Admiral'), with a maisonette-style modern interior, serves as a cocktail lounge.

27

28

29 30

27-42: 2階に設けられたミシュラン二つ星（1993年度）をもつレストラン「ラ・パルム・ドール（黄金のヤシ）」。80席。ビーチを眺望するバルコニーを付設する。ここは〝カンヌ映画祭〟に出席した世界的に有名な映画関係者の写真を飾ったレストラン。内装はアール・デコ様式が取り入れられ、使われる椅子は開業時にロンドンの名店ワーリング・アンド・ギローから搬入されたベルジェール（クッション付き安楽椅子）の複製品。27-29: レストラン専用につくられた2階のコリドール（写真右窓外側がプールサイド）には、アール・デコ様式のコンソール・テーブルや花形の壁ライトが使われる。

27-42: *La Palme d'Or* ('The Golden Palm') restaurant on the first floor earned two stars in the Michelin Guide (1993 edition). The restaurant seats 80 and has a balcony facing the beach. Hanging from the walls are photos of famous actors and other movie industry people who have visited the annual Cannes Film Festival. The Art Deco interior includes reproductions of the original *bergères* (cushioned armchairs) supplied by Waring & Gillow of London. 27-29: An Art Deco console table and flower-shaped wall lights in the first-floor corridor leading to the restaurant. (The window on the right of the photo overlooks the pool.)

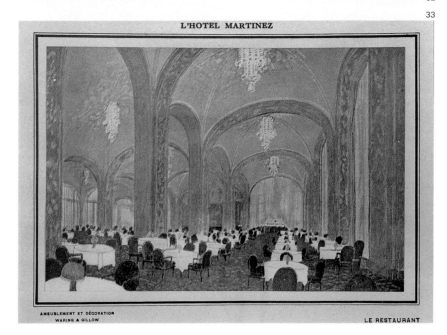

31: 1985年から総料理長を務めるクリスチャン・ヴィレー(中央)とレストラン・スタッフ。ヴィレーはアルザス生まれ。その長い料理経歴と料理の独創性から、このホテルを所有するコンコルド・ホテルズ・グループのグランド・シェフのひとり。ホテルで開催される"エスコフィエ・スタージュ(料理人の講習会)"の教師も務める。さらに彼は"料理アカデミー"の一員でもある。32: レストラン入口の「バー」エリアを飾るアール・デコ様式の時計とキャビネット。33: 開業時に設けられていた「ル・レストラン」(写真提供:ホテル・マルティネス)。34: メニューのカバー。35: "ヤマドリ茸のラヴィオリ田舎風"と名付けられた前菜。36: 古風なスタイルのフォア・グラの前菜。37: ホタテの前菜、トリュフと野菜のせんぎり添え。38: チョコレートでつくった小籠と栗のデザート。39: 柑橘類のゼリー・サヴァラン(王冠の形)風。40: 星形ケーキ、なんきん豆ソース。41: "エスキモーの雪小屋(イーグルー)"と名付けられたタイム味のデザート。42: 特注品の食器はベルナルドのリモージュ焼、デコール・エクスクリズィフ。

31: Chef de Cuisine Christian Willer (center) and the restaurant staff. Willer was born in the Alsace region, and has been the head chef here since 1985. In honor of his long years of service and the originality of his cooking style, the Concorde Hotels Group (the hotel's owner) has named him one of their Grand Chefs. Willer also teaches at the Escoffier Stage, a cooking course sponsored by the hotel, and is a member of the Académie Culinaire. 32: An Art Deco clock and cabinet stand in the *Bar* area near the restaurant entrance. 33: When the hotel first opened, guests could dine at *Le Restaurant* (photo courtesy of Hotel Martinez). 34: A menu cover. 35: Country-style ravioli with *cèpe* mushrooms (*les raviolis de gibiers au fumet de cèpes*). 36: Foie gras appetizer with chickpea crêpes (*lobe de foie gras préparé à l'ancienne, galettes de socca aux poireaux, rattes poivre et sel*). 37: Scallops with broccoli and julienned dried tomatoes (*coquilles st-jacques aux brocolis, julienne de tomates séchées sur clayette*). 38: Chocolate dessert with chestnut cream and marc sauce (*panier de chocolat à la crème de castagne, sauce au vieux marc de champagne*). 39: Savarin of jellied citrus fruits (*savarin d'agrumes en fine gelée, granité au vin de noix*). 40: Star-shaped cake with pistachio sauce (*constellation de gianduja en velours, sauce pistache*). 41: Pineapple "igloo" dessert flavored with thyme (*"Igloo" à l'ananas, rafraîchi au thym*). 42: The specially made servingware is *décor exclusif* Limoges china by Bernardaud.

35

36

37

38

39

40

41

42

43

44

45

AMEUBLEMENT & DÉCORATION
WARING & GILLOW

LA SALLE DES FÊTES

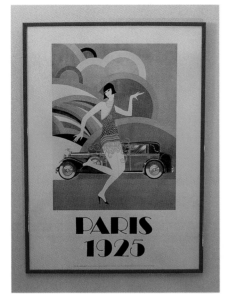

46

47

48

49

43,44: 12カ所設けられている集・宴会場のなかで最大の宴会場「リヴィエラ・サロン」とスタッフ。24×27m、総床面積650m²。レセプション形式で800名、バンケット形式で560名を収容する。この宴会場は「カリフォルニ・サロン」と「フロリド・サロン」に2等分割使用が可能な施設。45: ホテル開業時に設けられていた大天窓をもつ宴会場「ラ・サル・デ・フェート(祭りの大サロン)」。この宴会場は現存しない(イラスト提供:ホテル・マルティネス)。46: サロンの廊下を飾るポスター。47,48: 2階に新装された4カ所の小サロンのひとつ「シャガール・サロン」。49: レセプション形式にセッティングされた「クロワゼット・サロン」。18×19m、総床面積340m²。集・宴会場の総床面積は合計1,500m²にも及ぶ。

43, 44: The *Riviera Salon*, the largest of 12 meeting and banquet facilities, and its staff. The room measures 24 by 27 meters (79 by 89 feet), with a total area of 650 square meters (6,997 square feet). Capacity is 800 persons for receptions and 560 for banquets. The room can also be divided in half, creating the *Californie Salon* and the *Floride Salon*. 45: *La Salle des Fêtes*, lit by a large skylight, was one of the hotel's original banquet facilities. The room no longer exists. (Illustration courtesy of Hotel Martinez.) 46: A poster in the Salon corridor. 47, 48: The *Chagall Salon*, one of four newly redecorated small rooms on the first floor. 49: The *Croisette Salon*, set up for a reception. The room measures 18 by 19 meters (59 by 62 feet), with a total area of 340 square meters (3,660 square feet). Meeting and banquet facilities at the hotel add up to a total area of 1,500 square meters (16,146 square feet).

52

53

54

55

50-56: 15カ所設けられているスイート・ルームのひとつ「スイート(629-631号室)」。ここは応接間から両脇の寝室が使用可能。50,51: 各寝室は浴室を付設し、ツイン・ベッドの寝室とダブル・ベッドの寝室で構成。52: バスケットにセットされたウエルカム・フルーツ。53: ドアの部屋表示はアール・デコの文字デザイン。54,55: 応接間のカーテン・ロッド・カバー、暖炉、壁ライトなどはアール・デコ様式のデザインを取り入れ新しくつくられたもの。56: 開業時の部屋のイラスト(イラスト提供:ホテル・マルティネス)。家具、調度品はロンドンの名店ワーリンド・アンド・ギローから搬入された。

50–56: Suite 629–631, one of fifteen suites. Bedrooms on both sides of the sitting room may be used. 50, 51: The suite includes a double bedroom and a twin bedroom, each of which has an attached bathroom. 52: A welcome fruit basket. 53: Initials are incorportated in the Art Deco–style design of the door plate. 54, 55: The curtain rod cover, fireplace and wall lights in the sitting room are modern reproductions of classic Art Deco fixtures. 56: A guest room at the time the hotel opened (illustration courtesy of Hotel Martinez). The furnishings were supplied by Waring & Gillow, the famous London store.

56

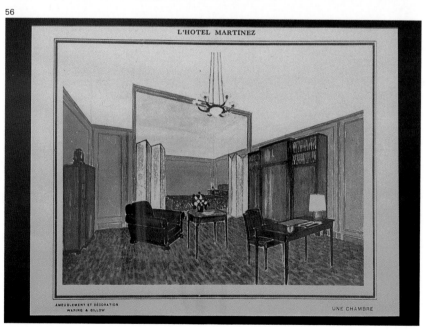

57

58

57,58: 窓側にシッティング・エリアを設けた「ジュニア・スイート(510号室)」。浴室はバスとシャワー・ブースを別にし、大理石の壁と床でコーディネート。59: 壁側に大きなワードローブを置いた「307号室」。この部屋は長期滞在者用につくられた。ベッドカバーとアームチェアーの生地は共布。60: カーテン、カーペット、壁をグリーン色で統一した「212号室」。アームチェアーとソファーは共布が使われている。開業時にホテルの内装がアール・デコ様式でコーディネートされていたことから、リノヴェーション時にこの様式デザインが家具、壁ライト、暖炉、カーテン・ロッド・カバーなどに取り入れられている。すべての部屋で仏・英・独語放送を含む計15チャンネルのテレビ放送が楽しめる。

59

57, 58: There is a sitting area next to the window in *Junior Suite 510*. The bathroom has marble walls and floor, and includes a separate bath and shower stall. 59: *Room 307*, for the use of long-term guests, has a large wardrobe next to the wall. The bedspreads and armchair upholstery use matching fabric. 60: *Room 212* has cream-colored curtains, carpeting and walls, and the armchairs and sofa are covered in matching fabric. The original hotel interior was Art Deco in style, so Art Deco furniture, wall lights, fireplaces, curtain rod covers, and so on were used during the renovation work. Fifteen channels of television are available in the guest rooms, with programming in French, English, German and other languages.

60

61

64

65

61-65: ブルーのカラー・スキームでジグザグ模様の壁紙、カーペット、家具を統一。ビーチを眺望する「ジュニア・スイート(312号室)」。62: 朝食のルーム・サービスには3種類のジャムが用意される。食器はベルナルドのリモージュ焼。63: 窓から望む早朝の海。カンヌは地中海を巡る豪華客船の寄港地でもある。64: ハウスキーパーのスーパーバイザー。65: バス・アメニテイは調香師アニック・グタル製。66: カーテンとベッドカバーを花柄の共布で統一した「405号室」。67: 最もスタンダード・タイプの部屋「325号室」。ホテルはバカンス期間の7〜8月がハイ・シーズン、4〜6月と9、10月がミッド・シーズンの料金設定。クリスマス、イースター、カンヌ映画祭などの期間は特別料金となる。

61-65: *Junior Suite 312*, looking out over the beach, has blue zigzag-patterned wallpaper, carpeting and furniture. 62: Room service breakfast comes with three flavors of jam. Serving-ware is Limoges china by Bernardaud. 63: A view of the early-morning sea from the window. Cannes is a popular port of call for luxury passenger ships cruising the Mediterranean. 64: A housekeeping supervisor. 65: Bathroom amenities are supplied by perfumer Annick Goutal. 66: Curtains and bedspreads in *Room 405* use matching floral-patterned fabric. 67: *Room 325*, the most common type of standard guest room. The hotel charges high season rates during July and August, and less expensive mid-season rates during April, May, June, September and October. Higher rates are in effect for the Christmas and Easter holidays and the Cannes Film Festival.

62

63

66

67

Carlton Inter·Continental Cannes

58, La Croisette, BP 155, 06406 Cannes Cedex, France

ビーチ・リゾート・カンヌを象徴する白亜のホテルとして名高い。20世紀初めまで使われていたホテル・ド・ラ・プラージュ（ビーチ・ホテルの意）を壊し、新ホテルが建てられた。このプロジェクトは、コート・ダジュールで多数のホテルを建設したデヴェロッパー＝ヘンリー・ルール最後の仕事だった。建設費の大半をロシア大公ウラディミールが出資。大公の委嘱により設計を建築家シャルル・デルマが担当。彼は当時の人気ダンサー＝ベル・オテロの豊満なバストをイメージし、2つのタワーを屋上に配した白い優美なホテルを完成させた。開業は1912年。1922年1月には国際連盟の会議を開催。1920年代終わりまでは冬季のみオープンするリゾート・ホテルとして、欧州の貴族や要人により最も華やかな一時代が築かれた。

　現在のホテルは、1946年9月20日から開催されている"カンヌ映画祭"で、各国の映画関係者が常泊するホテルとして世界に知られている。

This famous chalk-white hotel has become a well-known symbol of the beach resort of Cannes. The site was originally occupied by the Hotel de la Plage ('Beach Hotel'), which was torn down at the beginning of the century. The present hotel was the last project of Henry Ruhl, a developer who built a number of other hotels along the Côte d'Azur. Investment capital was provided by the Grand Duke Vladimir of Russia, who commissioned architect Charles Delmas to design the building. The plan includes two round towers on the roof; these were said to be inspired by the bust of the very popular Belle Otéro, a fabled dancer of the era. The hotel opened in 1912, and in January 1922 the first Supreme Council of the League of Nations was held here. Until the end of the 1920s the hotel was open only in wintertime; during its elegant heyday it served as a favorite winter resort of the European aristocracy.

Today the hotel is best known for its role each year during the Cannes Film Festival. Since the festival started in September 1946, this has been a popular lodging place for members of the international film community attending the festival.

1: 開業の1カ月後に投函されたポストカード。現在のホテル・ファサードと変わらない（ポストカード提供：カールトン・インター・コンチネンタル・カンヌ）。2: 最上階に設けられた美食レストラン「ラ・ベル・オテロ」のメニュー・カバー。ベル・エポック期の人気ダンサー＝ベル・オテロのダンス・シーンが描かれている。3: ミシュラン一つ星（1993年度）をもつ美食レストラン「ラ・コート」（P-88, P-89参照）。

1: A postcard dating from a month after the hotel opened; the façade of the hotel is still the same today (postcard courtesy of Carlton Inter·Continental Cannes). 2: A menu cover from the top-floor gourmet restaurant *La Belle Otéro* shows the popular Belle Epoque–era dancer after whom the restaurant was named. 3: The gourmet restaurant *La Côte* earned one star in the Michelin Guide (1993 edition; see also pages 88 and 89).

4

5

6

7

4: ダンサー=ベル・オテロの胸をイメージしたホテル両端のタワーのひとつ。5: 車寄せとして使われるポーチコ。時計を飾ったポーチコ屋上は、集会場のバルコニーとして使われる。6: 1922年1月、ホテルで開催された国際連盟の会議に出席した要人名を記したプレートが入口ファサードに飾られる。

この会議にイタリア人ジャーナリストとして参加していたB・ムッソリーニが、その騒がしい品行から追放されたエピソードが残っている。7: ホテルの総支配人クリスチャン・ル・プランス。ベルギー、ドイツ、アメリカ、オーストラリアを経て1988年から現職。8: 夏服のベルマン。9: 左が冬服のベルマン、右が冬

服のコンシェルジュ。10: 冬服の女性レセプション・スタッフのひとり。11: 「カフェ・カールトン」のスタッフ。

8

9

10

11

4: One of the two rooftop cupolas, inspired by the breasts of legendary dancer Belle Otéro. **5:** The portico is used as a vehicle entrance. The roof of the portico, which also serves as a balcony for the banquet area, has a large clock. **6:** A plaque in the entrance façade lists many of the famous figures who attended sessions of the League of Nations here in January 1922. Benito Mussolini, the Fascist leader who was soon to become Italian premier, attended the sessions as a journalist but was expelled for his disruptive conduct. **7:** General Manager Christian Le Prince worked in Belgium, Germany, America and Australia before coming here in 1988. **8:** Bellmen in summer uniform. **9:** A bellman (left) and concierge (right) in winter uniform. **10:** A female member of the reception staff in winter uniform. **11:** The staff of *Café Carlton.*

13

14

15

16

12-16: シッティング・エリアを設け大理石の円柱と床で飾られた「レセプション・ホール」。回転ドアの左側が木彫パネルでつくられた「コンシェルジュ・カウンター」、右側が「レセプション」。12: シッティング・エリアで使われる安楽椅子はルイ16世様式ベルジェールのデザインを取り入れ新しくつくられたもの。13: 2階に設けられた5カ所の「ミーティング・ルーム」へ通じる階段。写真右下が電話ブース、中央が「ゲスト・リレーションズ」のデスク、シャンデリアの奥が「コンシェルジュ・カウンター」。14: 「エントランス・ホール」では2種類のシャンデリアとランタン形のシャンデリアが使われる。15,16: 夏服の女性レセプション・スタッフと夏服のコンシェルジュ。

12–16: The *Reception Hall*, with marble floors and columns, includes a sitting area. To the left of the revolving door is the *Concierge Counter*, with carved wood panels, and to the right is the *Reception* desk. 12: New reproductions of Louis XVI *bergères* (easy chairs) furnish the sitting area. 13: A stairway leading to the five *Meeting Rooms* on the first floor (the level above the ground floor). Telephone booths are visible at the lower right of the photo, the *Guest Relations* desk is at the center, and the *Concierge Counter* is behind the chandelier. 14: Two types of chandeliers and lantern-style chandeliers light the *Entrance Hall*. 15,16: Female reception staff and concierges in summer uniform.

17

18

19

20

17,19:「エントランス・ホール」に設けられたバー「キャヴィア・クラブ」とメニュー・カバー。イランやロシア産など5種類のキャヴィアが常時用意される。18,20,21:「エントランス・ホール」に接続し広いスペースをもつ「ラウンジ」。中央に列柱（コロナード）を配した設計。22: ホテル1階の平面図。カンヌが初めて夏のリゾートとしてオープンしたのは1930年8月から。それまでのコート・ダジュールは、有名な"ブリュ列車"で訪れるイギリス人たちの冬季リゾートとして賑わっていた。夏の猛烈な暑さは彼等のフィーリングに合わなかったからである。しかし、このホテルも1930年の夏には営業を開始。スカンジナビアやイタリアの貴族、ドイツやスウェーデンの王族、インドのマハラジャたちが集い、英国式ライフ・スタイルのエレガントなリゾート・ホテルとして名を高めた。

17, 19: The *Caviar Club* bar, in the *Entrance Hall*, and a menu cover. Five varieties of caviar, including Iranian and Russian, are available. 18, 20, 21: Next to the *Entrance Hall* is the spacious *Lounge*, with a row of columns at its center. 22: A floor plan of the ground floor. In August 1930 this became the first Cannes resort hotel to stay open for the summer. Before then the area was a popular winter resort for vacationers from England, who arrived via the famous "Train Bleu." Somehow, the fierce heat of summer didn't suit the temperament of its English visitors. Beginning in 1930, though, the hotel began attracting a new summertime clientele, as Scandinavian and Italian aristocrats, members of the German and Swedish royalty, and Indian Maharajahs all gathered here to enjoy a summer resort with elegant English-style service.

21

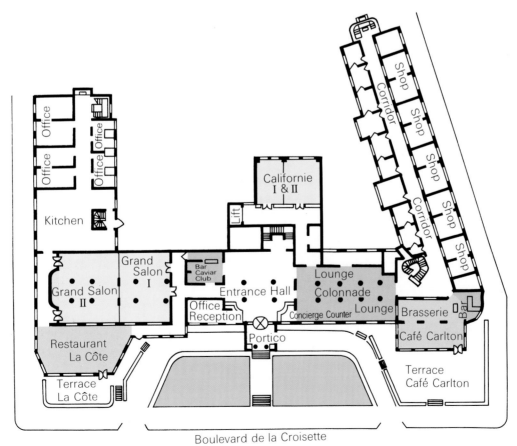

22

Boulevard de la Croisette

23

24

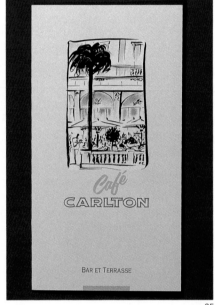

25

26

27

28

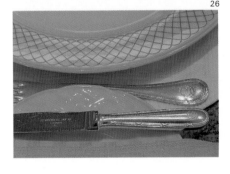

23–28: 夏季にテラス席を設けることから"ファッショナブル・ブラスリー"と命名した「カフェ・カールトン」。23: 入口に置かれた同名の小さな「バー」。24: 「カフェ・カールトン」の入口付近。クラシックな階段が残され、カンヌ映画祭の古い写真が壁を飾る。25: メニュー・カバー。26: 食器はベルナルドのリモージュ焼、銀製品はクリストフル。27: レストラン・マネージャーとスタッフ。

23–28: The *Café Carlton*, nicknamed the "Fashionable Brasserie," has terrace seating in the summer. 23: A small bar is located near the entrance. 24: The entrance area of *Café Carlton* includes an old-fashioned staircase, and old photos from the Cannes Film Festival hang from the walls. 25: A menu cover. 26: Servingware is Limoges china by Bernardaud, and the silverware is by Cristofle. 27: The restaurant manager and staff.

29

30

31

32

33

34

35

36

37

29-37: テラスを設けた美食レストラン「ラ・コート」。ドーム形のガラス天窓で飾られている。30: 1986年5月から総料理長を務めるスィルヴァン・デュパック。アヌシーの叔父のホテルを振出しに、ヴィッシーのホテル・アルベール1世、シャトー・ダルティニー(ホテル)などを経て現職。31: メニュー・カバー。32: スズキのバリグール・ソース(ちょうせんあざみの調理法)。33: 牛の心臓肉のフライ、茸とエシャロット添え。34: 大きいランゴスチーヌのデリー風スパイシー・ソース。35: 卵黄ケーキとアイスクリームのデザート。36: ヘッド・ソムリエのR・F・ドラ。1957年からホテルに勤務するベテラン。37: 食器はドイツ製のボーシャーから、1991年に特註のクリストフル製アリゼ・デザイン、デコール・イナルテラブルに替えられた。

29-37: *La Côte* gourmet restaurant includes a terrace and dome-shaped glass skylights. 30: Chef de Cuisine Sylvain Dupark trained at his uncle's hotel in Annecy, then worked at the Hotel Albert 1er in Vichy and the Château d'Artigny (hotel) before starting here in May 1986. 31: A menu cover. 32: Sea bass with artichokes (*barigoule de loup de petite pêche aux artichauts violets*). 33: Fried beef hearts with mushrooms and shallots (*coeur de filet de boeuf poêlé aux échalotes grises*). 34: Dublin bay prawn with spicy sauce Delhi-style (*bouquet de grosses langoustines aux épices de Delhi*). 35: Zabaglione and ice cream dessert (*sabayon de miel au mascarata en velours cacao*). 36: Head Sommelier Robert Fresia Dolla has been here since 1957. 37: In 1991 the

German Bauscher china was replaced by specially made *décor inaltérable* "Alize's design" servingware from Cristofle.

WITHDRAWN-UN

39

42

38

40

41

43

38-41: 最大の宴会場「グランド・サロンⅡ」。ここは「グランド・サロンⅠ」をつなぐ設計が取り入れられている。ⅠとⅡ合わせて、15.5×23.5m、総床面積360㎡。バンケット形式で280〜300人、レセプション形式で500人を収容する。39: 子供の裸体を描いた円形の天井照明用吊りライト。40: ドーム天井内部のフレスコ画。41: シャンデリアに付けられた羊の頭部彫刻。42: 壁ライトはジランドール（枝付き飾り燭台）のデザインを模し、羊彫刻が付けられた特註品。43: 1930年頃のホテル外景（写真提供：カールトン・インター・コンチネンタル・カンヌ）。44: ハウスキーパーとハウスキーパーのスーパーバイザー。45: 男性のハウスキーパー。46:「カフェ・カールトン」入口付近の階段室。47: ホテルの中央階段室。

38–41: *Grand Salon II*, the largest banquet room here, can be connected to *Grand Salon I*. Together, the two rooms measure 15.5 by 23.5 meters (51 by 77 feet), with a total area of 360 square meters (3,898 square feet). Total capacity is 280–300 persons for banquets and up to 500 for receptions. **39:** An unusual lighting fixture with a painting of naked children hangs from the ceiling. **40:** A fresco painting on the dome ceiling. **41:** Ram's head carvings adorn the chandeliers. **42:** The specially made girandole-style wall lights also have carved ram's heads. **43:** An exterior view of the hotel around 1930 (photo courtesy of Carlton Inter·Continental Cannes). **44:** A housekeeper and a housekeeping supervisor. **45:** A male housekeeper. **46:** The staircase at the entrance to *Café Carlton*. **47:** The hotel's central staircase.

44

45

46

47

48

49

48-61: 57室設けられている「スイート」の中で最高級の「スイート・アンペリアル」。ここは1988年のリノヴェーションで最上階に設けられた「スイート」。応接間、会議室兼食堂、書斎、3カ所の寝室、3カ所の浴室、長いバルコニーで構成される。48,49: 応接間と会議室兼食堂。50,51: 主寝室と書斎。1940年、カンヌは独裁者ムッソリーニの軍隊に包囲されるが、ホテルの営業は継続された。しかし、第2次世界大戦中の1944年6月ついにホテルを閉鎖。戦後、アメリカ軍指令部のスタッフ・ハウスとして約1年間使用された歴史をもつ。その後、1946年から開催されている"カンヌ映画祭"で世界の映画関係者が宿泊するホテルとして名を高めた。1970～1973年にはホテルを閉館せずリノヴェーションを慣行。1988年、西武セゾン・グループとスカンジナビア航空がホテルを買収。後に西武セゾン・グループが所有するインター・コンチネンタル・ホテルズに所有権が譲渡された。現在、500名の従業員が働くホテルとなっている。尚、ホテルの名称である"カールトン"とはスカンジナビア地域を語源とする言葉で"自由な人々の町"を意味する。

50

51

48–61: The *Suite Impériale*, the most luxurious of the hotel's 57 suite, was built on the top floor during the hotel's 1988 renovation. It includes a sitting room, a combination meeting/dining room, a library, three bedrooms, three bathrooms and a long balcony. 48, 49: The sitting room and meeting/dining room. 50, 51: The master bedroom and library. Although the hotel remained open in 1940 when Cannes was surrounded by Mussolini's troops, it closed in June 1944 toward the end of World War II. After the war it was used as a staff house for the American military command for about a year. After that it became famous as a lodging place for members of the movie industry, who came from around the world to attend the Cannes Film Festival beginning in 1946. From 1970 through 1973 the hotel was renovated while it remained open. In 1988 it was bought by the Japanese Seibu Saison Group and the Scandinavian Airline company, SAS; it was then transferred to Inter·Continental Hotels, which is owned by Seibu Saison Group. At present there is a staff of 500. The hotel's name is Scandinavian in origin; it means 'city of free men.'

52

53

54

55

52-61：「スイート・アンペリアル」。52：ルイ16世様式フォートイユ（肘掛椅子）を置いた寝室のひとつ。53：花柄のベッドカバーとカーテンを共布にした寝室のひとつ。54,55：ジャクージー付きバスタブを備えた主浴室。バスタブ後方にトイレとシャワー・ブースが設けられ、クラシック・スタイルの洗面台が2カ所置かれている。56：バス・アメニテイ。57：ウエルカム・シャンペンやウエルカム・フルーツを運ぶルームサービスのスタッフ。58：ナイト・テーブルにセットされた電話とメモ用紙。マッチや電話案内帳にもホテルの建物イラストが描かれている。59,60：最上階のコーナーに設けられた「スイート・アンペリアル」の長いバルコニー。ホテル専用埠頭やカンヌのビーチを一望する。61：朝食用ドアタッグ。裏はフランス語で表記されている。

52-61: The *Suite Impériale*. 52: One of the bedrooms, furnished with Louis XVI *fauteuils* (armchairs). 53: One of the bedrooms, with matching floral-patterned fabric used for the bedspreads and curtains. 54, 55: The main bathroom includes a large bathtub with jacuzzi. Behind the bathtub are a toilet and shower stall; the room also has two old-fashioned sinks. 56: Bathroom amenities. 57: Room service staff delivers a welcome bottle of champagne and a welcome fruit basket. 58: A telephone and memo pad on the night table. A painting of the hotel also appears on the matchbooks and telephone directory. 59, 60: The *Suite Impériale* occupies a corner of the top floor, and includes a long balcony with a view of the beach and the hotel's pier. 61: A breakfast door tag. The other side of the tag is written in French.

56

57

58

59

60

61

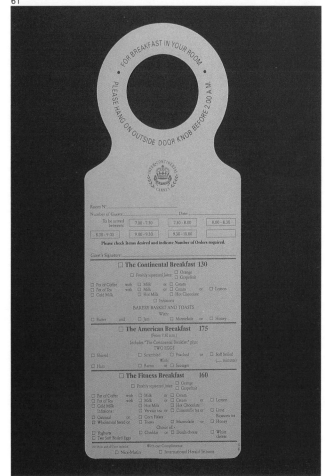

62

63

64

65

66

67

68

62-68: 建物前面のコーナー部分に応接間を置き、両脇に2カ所の寝室を設けた「コーナー・スイート（641号室）」。62,63: 応接間のコーナーに置かれるデスクや安楽椅子、アルムワール（両開き衣裳箪笥）はルイ15世様式のデザインを取り入れ新しく製作されたもの。鍍金鏡もルイ15世様式のデザイン。64: 応接間に通じる入口からの廊下。ルイ16世様式半円形コモードは複製品。65: 入口ドア枠外部を飾る怪魚の漆喰彫刻。66: 小バルコニーから望むカンヌのビーチ。夏にはビーチに「カールトン・ビーチ・レストラン」が開店する。67: ベッドカバーとカーテンを共布にした寝室のひとつ。68: カーテン、布壁、ヘッドボード、クッションをピンクの共布で統一した寝室。浴室は大きなワードローブを設けている。

62–68: The drawing room of *Corner Suite (641)* occupies a corner at the front of the building, with bedrooms on either side. 62, 63: The desk and easy chairs in the corner of the drawing room, the armoire, and the gilt mirror are all newly made Louis XV reproductions. 64: A hall-way leading to the drawing room from the entrance. The Louis XVI–style semi-circular commode is a reproduction. 65: The outside of the entrance door frame has plaster carvings of monstrous fish. 66: The beach at Cannes, seen from the small balcony. The *Carlton Beach Restaurant* is open on the beach every summer. 67: Matching fabric is used for the bedspreads and curtains in this bedroom. 68: Matching pink fabric is used for the curtains, walls, headboard and cushions in one of the bedrooms. The bathroom includes a large wardrobe.

69

72

73

70

71

69: 中央エレヴェーターの6階ウエイティング・エリア。ルイ15世様式フォートイユとルイ16世様式コモードが置かれる。写真中央左側（両開きドアの左前部）が中央階段室、両開きドア奥に部屋用の通廊が設けられている。70: 中央階段室の各フロアーから部屋用の通廊に抜ける両開きのドア。写真は5階。71: 各階の通廊では布壁の色が変えられている。写真は6階。72: 部屋の入口ドア裏に張られた緊急避難用の平面図。73,74: 海側に置かれた最も人気が高いスタンダードの部屋「526号室」。75: ホテルの両脇に置かれた〝サイド・ビュー・ルーム〟とも呼ばれる「521号室」。中国趣味の絵画と壁紙で飾られ、備え付けの大きなワードローブをもつ。

69: The central elevator waiting area on the fifth floor has Louis XV *fauteuils* and a Louis XVI commode. To the left of the center of the photo (to the front and left of the double doors) is the central stairway. Beyond the double doors is a corridor leading to the guest rooms. 70: On each floor a set of double doors separates the central stairway from a corridor leading to the guest rooms. The fourth floor is shown here. 71: A different color of fabric is used in the corridor on each floor. The fifth floor is shown here. 72: A floor plan showing emergency exit routes is posted on the back of each guest room door. 73, 74: *Room 526*, facing the ocean, is the most popular type of standard room. 75: *Room 521* is called a "side view room," and is located on one side of the hotel. Furnishings include chinois paintings and wallpaper and a large wardrobe.

74

75

76

76-88: 1988年、ホテル最上階にオープンした「カールトン・カジノ・クラブ」。このクラブはカジノ、レストラン、バー、ダンス・フロアーなどで構成される。ここは完成までに4カ月の工期と約42億円が投下された。**76-79:** カジノにはルーレットやブラック・ジャックのテーブルが15台用意されている。ドーム型の天井にはフレスコ画が描かれ、ヴェネチア製シャンデリアや壁ライトで装飾されている。この「カールトン・カジノ・クラブ」はロンドンに本部を置くロンドン・クラブス・リミテッドにより運営されている。

76-88: The *Carlton Casino Club*, which opened on the top floor in 1988, includes a casino, restaurant, bar and dance floor. Construction of the club took four months and cost approximately 140 million French francs. **76-79:** The casino features 15 roulette and black-jack tables. There is a dome-shaped ceiling with a fresco painting, Venetian-made chandeliers, and wall lights. The *Carlton Casino Club* is managed by London Clubs Limited, headquartered in London.

77

78

80

81

82

83

84

85

80-88：「カールトン・カジノ・クラブ」に設けられた
ミシュラン二つ星（1993年度）の美食レストラン
「ラ・ベル・オテロ」。ミシュラン三つ星（1992年度）
のレストラン「ムーラン・ド・ムージャン」で9年間修業
したフランシス・ショヴォーが総料理長。80：オマー
ル・エビのブルターニュ風、ニース産野菜添え、バリ
グール・ソース。81：仔牛のフィレ・ミニョン、野菜の
みじん切り添え、オーソ・ブッコ・ソース。82：ラング
スチーヌ、ホタテ、フォアグラを添えた温サラダ。83：
新鮮なフルーツのデザート、フルーツ・ソース。84：
食器はカジノのフレスコ天井画を絵付けした特注
品のリモージュ焼、デコール・イナルテラブル。85：
このレストランの名称ともなった人気ダンサー＝ベ
ル・オテロの肖像画が飾られる。86,87：レストラン
のダイニング・エリア。88：ビーチを一望するバル

コニーも付設されている。スー・シェフのJ・L・オーテ
ュとレストラン・スタッフ。89：ホテル専用埠頭から
見たホテルの夜景。

80-88: *La Belle Otéro* gourmet restaurant,
inside the *Carlton Casino Club*, earned two stars
in the Michelin Guide (1993 edition). Chef de
Cuisine Francis Chauveau trained for nine years
in the three-star restaurant (1992 edition) *Le
Moulin de Mougins* before coming here. 80:
Lobster Breton-style with vegetables Niçois and
artichoke sauce (*rosace de homard Breton aux
artichauts violets, jus barigoule aux légumes
Niçois*). 81: Veal filet mignon with diced vegetables and osso bucco sauce (*filet mignon de
veau fermier en jus d'osso-bucco, galette de

tagliatelles au Porme*). 82: Warm salad of Dublin Bay prawn, scallops with carrots, and foie
gras with apples (*composé de langoustines en
vinaigrette de poireaux, Saint-Jacques aux
carottes fondantes, croustillant de foie gras aux
reinettes*). 83: Fresh fruit dessert with fruit
sauce (*fraîcheur de fruits exotiques en coulis de
mangues, sorbets cacao, noix de coco*). 84:
The servingware is specially made *décor
inaltérable* Limoges china showing the fresco
painting from the casino ceiling. 85: A portrait of
dancer Belle Otéro, after whom the restaurant is
named. 86, 87: The restaurant dining area. 88:
The restaurant has a balcony with a view of the
beach. Sous chef Jean-Luc Ortu and the restaurant staff. 89: A nighttime view of the hotel
from the hotel's pier.

86

87

88

Le Château du Domaine Saint-Martin

Avenue des Templiers, 06140 Vence, France

　ニースやアンティーブ半島の海岸線まで眺望する絶好の丘陵地に建つホテル。ホテルの名称は、紀元350年にトゥールの司教サン・マルタンが布教に当地を訪れたことに由来する。1115年、エルサレムから戻ったテンプル騎士団にプロヴァンス伯爵が領地の防衛を条件に現在のホテルの敷地を与え、城塞が築かれた。

　1936年、現在のオーナーであるジュネーヴ家が16ヘクタールにも及ぶこの敷地を購入。城塞跡を残して邸宅が建てられた。1957年には邸宅をホテルに改築。翌年開業したホテルには、西ドイツ首相アデナウアーやアメリカ大統領トルーマンが滞在。当初VIP用のホテルとして利用された。その後、数回の改装で本館とは別に10棟のヴィラとコテージを増設。邸宅時代に収集されたアンティーク家具が惜しげもなく、パブリック・エリアや部屋に使われている。またここは、優良なサービスから世界中のリピーターが集う小型ホテルとして知られている。

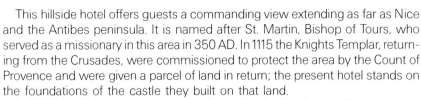

This hillside hotel offers guests a commanding view extending as far as Nice and the Antibes peninsula. It is named after St. Martin, Bishop of Tours, who served as a missionary in this area in 350 AD. In 1115 the Knights Templar, returning from the Crusades, were commissioned to protect the area by the Count of Provence and were given a parcel of land in return; the present hotel stands on the foundations of the castle they built on that land.

In 1936 the 16-hectare site was purchased by the Genève family, the current owners. They built a mansion on the castle foundations, and in 1957 the mansion was converted to use as a hotel. Opening the following year, the new hotel hosted a number of VIPs, including German Prime Minister Konrad Adenauer and US President Harry Truman. In the following years numerous renovations were carried out and ten separate villas and cottages were added in addition to the main wing. Today the hotel attracts many repeat visitors from around the world with its excellent service and its beautiful interiors, which are filled with rare antique furnishings dating back to the hotel's days as a private mansion.

1：海抜500mの丘陵に建てられた本館全景。本館の回りに5カ所のヴィラ、本館から離れた岩山の中腹に5カ所のコテージをもつ。2：レストランの灰皿に使われる司教サン・マルタンのロゴ・マーク。3：風除室の壁を飾る司教サン・マルタン像。これは17世紀に製作されたもの。4：ストライプの日除けを設けた「レストラン」。ミシュラン一つ星（1993年度）をもつコート・ダジュールでも人気のレストランである。

1: A view of the main wing, built on a hillside site 500 meters above sea level. There are five villas around the main wing, and five cottages further away, on a nearby mountainside. 2: The image of Saint Martin, Bishop of Tours, is used on the restaurant ashtrays. 3: The vestibule wall has a seventeenth-century statue of Saint Martin. 4: The *Restaurant* can be identified by its striped awnings. Popular with diners from all along the Côte d'Azur, it earned one star in the Michelin Guide (1993 edition).

5

6

7

5: コテージのヴェランダから眺望するホテル本館（写真右）とコート・ダジュールの海岸線。写真左下が中世からの町ヴァンス、その右上がアンティーブ半島。晴れた日には左にイタリア国境近くの街マントンから、右はサン・ラファエルまでを見渡せる絶好の立地に立つホテルである。6,7: 本館から続く敷地内に設けられたテニス・コートと屋外プール。岩山の中腹にコテージが見える。夏季にはプール・サイドにレストランがオープンしバーベキューが楽しめる。8,9: 12世紀に駐屯したテンプル騎士団が造ったといわれる城塞跡（ハネ橋の橋脚）が保存されている。このテンプル騎士団が敷地内に〝黄金の山羊像〟を埋めたという伝説が現在も語り伝えられている。

5: The main wing (at right) and the Côte d'Azur shoreline, seen from the veranda of one of the cottages. At the lower left of the photo is the village of Vence, populated since medieval times, and to the upper right of the village is the Antibes peninsula. On clear days the hotel commands a spectacular view stretching from the town of Menton, near the Italian border (to the left), all the way to St. Raphaël (to the right). 6, 7: Continuing in a straight line from the main wing, one comes to a tennis court and an outdoor pool within the grounds. The cottages can be seen on the mountainside. During summer months guests can enjoy a barbecue at the poolside restaurant. 8, 9: The pier of a bridge is preserved among the ruins of the castle where the Knights Templar were said to have been stationed in the twelfth century. According to a legend still in circulation today the Knights Templar buried a statue of a "Golden Goat" somewhere on the grounds.

10

13

14

11

12

10: 道路から見たホテル入口付近。左側の建物裏と写真右奥に本館宿泊者用の駐車場を完備。写真右奥下部に5カ所のヴィラがある。ヴィラ宿泊者はヴィラ専用駐車場が使用できる。11, 13: 本館入口に設けられた三角形のポーチコ。12: 白い漆喰壁と石の手摺で統一された階段室。踊り場にアンティークの家具が置かれている。14: 9年間コンシェルジュを務めるV・サイプレス。15: プロヴァンス風に建てられた本館。左側のタワー(城塞跡)内部の螺旋階段をそのまま利用し部屋が付設されている。本館には計14室の部屋が設けられ、そのうちの1カ所のみが「アパートメント(スイート)」として使われている。16: 本館1階の平面図。

10: The hotel entrance area, seen from the road. Parking areas for guests staying in the main wing are visible behind the building at the left and also at the far right of the photo. The five villas are at the far lower right. There is a separate parking area for guests staying in the villas. 11, 13: The entrance to the main wing includes a triangular portico. 12: The staircase has white plaster walls and stone banisters, with antique furniture on the landings. 14: Vincent Cypres has worked as concierge here for nine years. 15: The main wing was built in Provençal style. The left-hand tower, part of the castle ruins, houses a guest room which is reached by spiral staircase. The main wing has a total of 14 guest rooms, including just one *Appartment* (Suite). 16: A floor plan of the main wing's ground floor.

15

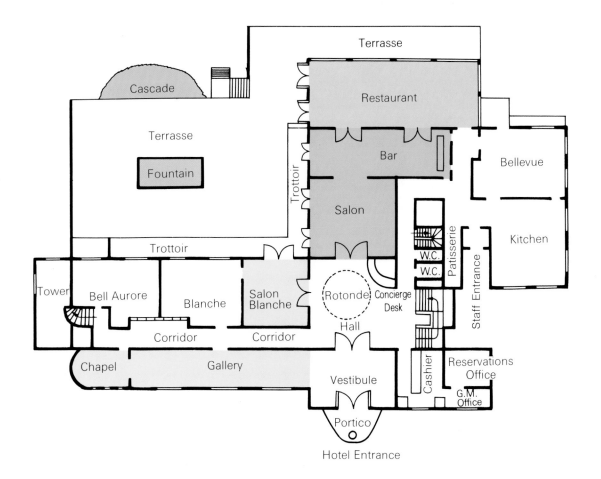

16

17

18

19

20

21

22

23

17：1958年に約1カ月滞在したアメリカ合衆国大統領トルーマン。18：1958年10月に滞在した当時の西ドイツ首相アデナウアー。19：前フランス大統領G・デスタンと西ドイツ首相シュミット。ホテルで行なわれた会議後の昼食スナップ。20：ホールに飾られる先代のオーナー、ダニエル・ジュネーヴの半身像。21：現在のオーナー、エドゥワール・ジュネーヴとパリ市長シラク（17-21の写真提供：ル・シャトー・デュ・ドメーヌ・サン・マルタン）。22：1967年からマネージャーを務めるA・ブルネ。彼女は1989年と1990年に、アメリカのトラベル・ダイ

ジェスト社が選ぶ "世界のベスト・ホテリエ50人" のひとりに選ばれたベテラン。23-26：本館1階に「チャペル」を設けた「ギャラリー」。イスラエル製カンデラーブラ、ルイ16世様式デスクなどで飾られている。

17: American President Harry Truman stayed here for an entire month in 1958. 18: German Prime Minister Konrad Adenauer stayed here in October 1958. 19: Former French President Valery Giscard d'Estaing and German Prime Minister Helmut Schmidt. The photo was taken at lunch, after a meeting at the hotel. 20: The

hall contains a bust of Daniel Genève, a previous owner. 21: The hotel's current owner, Edouard Genève, and Paris Mayor Jacques Chirac (photos no. 17–21 courtesy of Le Château du Domaine Saint-Martin). 22: Andrée Brunet has been manager here since 1967. In 1989 and 1990 she was named one of the "World's 50 Best Hoteliers" by Travel Digest Publications, an American company. 23–26: The *Chapel*, in the ground-floor *Gallery* in the main wing, includes an Israeli candelabrum and a Louis XVI desk.

24

25

26

27

28

29

30

31

27-32: 貴重なアンティークで飾られた「サロン」。ここはロビー・ラウンジの機能をもつ。**28**: 1700年代につくられたルイ15世様式コモード。ブロンズ像は後期ロココ彫刻を代表する彫刻家クロディオン(1738-1814年)が制作したもの。飾り枠付き掛時計(カルテル)はルイ15世様式。これはルイ15世時代に流行したロカイユ様式ともいわれる。**29**: ルイ15世様式フォートイユ(肘掛け椅子)とイタリア製ルネサンス時代のヴィトリーネ(ショーケース)。**30**: 暖炉上の人形ランプは17世紀のイタリア製。

31: ルイ15世様式デスク。これは18世紀に製作された。**32**: 17世紀に製作されたポルトガル製キャビネット。**33**: 「サロン・ブランシュ」にはルイ15世様式アルムワール(洋服箪笥)、珍しいルイ13世様式テーブルが使われている。**34**: ホール(ロトンド)2階の壁を飾るペルシャ製の絨毯。**35**: コテージ「サン・ランベール」の応接間で使われる1801年製のアルムワール。これはイタリア製と思われる。

32

33

34

35

27–32: The *Salon*, furnished with precious antiques, serves as the lobby lounge. 28: The Louis XV commode dates back to the 1700s. The bronze statue was made by Clodion (1738–1814), a noted late Rococo period sculptor. The *cartel* (wall clock) with decorative frame is a Louis XV piece. This style is also known as Rocaille, and was popular during the era of Louis XV. 29: A Louis XV *fauteuil* (upholstered armchair) and an Italian-made Renaissance-period vitrine. 30: Above the fireplace is a pair of seventeenth-century Italian figurine lamps. 31: This Louis XV desk was made in the eighteenth century. 32: A seventeenth-century Portuguese cabinet. 33: The *Salon Blanche* contains a Louis XV armoire and an unusual Louis XIII table. 34: A Persian carpet hangs from the first-floor wall of the Hall (Rotonda). 35: The armoire in the sitting room of *St. Lambert* cottage was made in 1801, probably in Italy.

36

37

38

39   40

36-47: ミシュラン一つ星（1993年度）の「レストラン」。夏季には外のテラスも利用される。36: トリュフ入りズッキーニの花の前菜。37: イトヨリのフィレと生野菜。38: 羊肉のういきょう添え。39,44: グラス、食器や灰皿にもサン・マルタンのロゴ・マークが入れられている。食器はドイツ製ボーシャー。41: フォアグラのサラダ、ホウレンソウとえぞイチゴ添え。42: えぞイチゴのミルフィユ。43: チョコレートのムース。ホテルまでは、ニース国際空港から約20kmの距離に位置するが、眺望の素晴らしさ、良質のサービス、料理の素晴らしさから、特に外来者が訪れる人気のレストランとして知られている。

41

42

43

44

36–47: The *Restaurant* earned one star in the Michelin Guide (1993 edition). There is also an outdoor terrace for dining in summer. **36:** Zucchini flowers with truffles (*fleurs de courgettes aux truffes*). **37:** Filet of mullet with herb vinaigrette (*filets de rougets du pays en verdurette*). **38:** Rack of lamb in casserole, flavored with fennel (*carré d'agneau en cocotte au fenouil*). **39, 44:** The glasses, china and ashtrays all feature the Saint Martin logo. The servingware was made in Germany by Bauscher. **41:** Salad of duck liver with spinach and raspberries (*salade de foie de canard aux épinards et aux framboises*). **42:** Raspberry mille-feuille pastry (*croustillant aux framboises*). **43:** Pear in wine with bitter chocolate mousse (*poire au vin et mousse de chocolat amer*). Although the hotel is some twenty kilometers from Nice International Airport, the restaurant still draws many diners from outside the hotel with its beautiful views, elegant service and excellent food.

45

46

47

48

49

45: 1975年から総料理長を務めるドミニク・フェ
リエールと彼のスタッフ。フェリエールは1947年生
まれ。彼の父親も名料理長だった。1967年、海軍
に務めた後、ビアリッツのカフェ・ド・パリ（ミシュラン
二つ星）、オッシュのホテル・ド・フランス（ミシュラン
二つ星）の料理長A・ダギャンのもとで修業。ロンド
ンのザ・サヴォイ（ホテル）やザ・バークレイ（ホテル）
に勤務した経歴をもつ。46:「レストラン」のサービ
ス・スタッフ。左から2人目がコート・ダジュール及び
プロヴァンス地域で、1976年度ベスト・メートル・
ドテルに選ばれたルネ・ルルー。彼はプロヴァンス地
域ソムリエ協会会長職とワインの講師も務める。
47: 朝食はテラスでも楽しめる。48,50: 中央に

噴水を配した「テラス」。49,51: スコッチ・モルト・
ウィスキーを数十種類取り揃えた「バー」。バーマン
はE・アンリィ。一般的に宿泊客の朝食はここで提
供される。

45: Dominique Ferriere, Chef de Cuisine since
1975, and the kitchen staff. Ferriere was born in
1947, the son of another famous chef. Starting
in 1967, after a tour in the Navy, he trained under
André Daguin of the two-star *Café de Paris* in
Biarritz and the two-star *Hotel de France* in
Auch. He also worked at two London hotels, The
Savoy and The Berkeley. 46: The *Restaurant*
service staff. Second from left is head sommeli-

er René Le Roux. In 1976 Le Roux was chosen as
the top maître d'hôtel in the Provence and Côte
d'Azur region. He is also president of a Provence
sommelier group as well as a teacher on the
subject of wine. 47: The *Terrasse* also serves
breakfast. 48, 50: A fountain stands at the center of the *Terrasse*. 49, 51: The *Bar*, and Barman
Erick Henri. Dozens of types of Scotch malt
whisky are available. Breakfast for hotel guests
is also served here.

50

51

52

55

53

54

56

52-56: 岩山の中腹に5カ所置かれているコテージのひとつ「ポナン(西)」。応接間、寝室、浴室、化粧室、ヴェランダから構成されている。ゲストの希望により、朝食やルームサービスも本館から運ばれる。応接間で使われるビュッフェ(食器戸棚)は19世紀製と思われる。寝室に置かれるテーブルはペンブルック・テーブルと呼ばれる。これは両翼が折り曲げられるデザインからバタフライ・テーブルの別名をもつ17世紀製。57-59: 本館の横に点在する2階建のヴィラ上階に位置する「レゾワ(鳥)」。プライヴェート・ロビー、応接間、寝室、バルコニー、化粧室、浴室から構成される。59: 応接間に飾られる小引出し付き机はルイ15世様式スクレテールと呼ばれる。

52–56: *Ponant* ('West'), one of five mountain-side cottages, contains a sitting room, bedroom, bathroom, powder room and veranda. Breakfast can be ordered through room service from the main wing. The buffet in the sitting room is believed to be a nineteenth-century antique. The seventeenth-century table in the bedroom is known as a Pembroke table; it is also called a butterfly table because of the curved design of the two wings. 57–59: *Les Oiseaux* ('The Birds'), in one of the two-story villas scattered around the main wing, contains a private lobby, sitting room, bedroom, balcony, powder room and bathroom. 59: The Louis XV desk with small drawers in the sitting room is called a *secrétaire*.

57

58

59

60

61

62

63

64

65

66

67

60: 本館タワー3階の部屋「プレフェレ（お気に入り）」。61,65: 本館タワー2階の部屋「ベアティテュード（至福）」で使われるナポレオン3世ボノル・デュ・ジュール（婦人用デスク）。これはライティング・デスクの一種類で赤べっ甲の表面に真鍮を象眼した19世紀中期製。62-64,66,67: 本館1階の部屋「ブランシュ」。ルイ9世の摂政となり南仏の支配を強化したルイ8世の王妃ブランシュ・ド・カスティーユ（1188〜1252年）から名が取られている。62: 上部に鳥と葡萄の彫刻を飾った珍しいルイ15世様式アルムワール。63: ルイ16世様式マルケトリー・コモード。ジュネーヴ家の邸宅時代に集められた膨大なアンティーク家具、広大な敷地に25室の部屋、一級のサービスと料理。そして、邸宅の気品を現在も留める雰囲気がこのホテル最大の魅力である。

60: *Préferée* ('Favorite') is a room on the second floor of the main wing tower. 61, 65: A Napoléon III *bonheur-du-jour* (ladies' writing desk) furnishes *Béatitude* ('Bliss'), a room on the first floor of the main wing tower. The desk was made in the mid-nineteenth century, and has a red tortoise-shell surface with brass inlay. 62–64, 66, 67: *Blanche* is a room on the ground floor of the main wing. It is named after Blanche de Castille (1188–1252), the wife of Louis VIII. Acting as regent for her son Louis IX when he was a child, she greatly strengthened government control over the south of France. 62: The upper portion of this unusual Louis XV armoire has carvings of birds and grapevines. 63: A Louis XVI marquetry commode. A great many antiques from the Genève family mansion are still used today. The hotel also has vast grounds, a small scale (only 25 guest rooms), excellent service and first-rate cuisine. Together, these features help establish the dignified, family mansion-style atmosphere that is one of the hotel's most charming qualities.

Le Saint-Paul

86, Rue Grande, 06570 Saint-Paul-de-Vence, France

1016年にはすでにコミュニティが形成されていたと記録に残る小高い峰の村サン・ポール・ド・ヴァンス。この美しい中世のたたずまいを色濃く残す人口2,000人あまりの村につくられたホテルである。現在のホテルの建物は、16世紀に建てられたファサードを保存したもの。

開業は1989年6月。1991年には現在のオーナーに買収されリノヴェーションを終え19室のホテルとなった。全室のインテリアはプロヴァンス様式で整えられ、ファブリックは"スーレアドォ"と呼ばれる独特のデザイン。これは当地のインテリア・デザイナー、ジャン・ディーヴのアイディア。この時レストランが増設され、壁に美しい花園で飾られた中庭の"トロンプ・ルイユ（だまし絵）"が描かれた。開業まもないホテルでありながら、20名のスタッフが心暖まるプロヴァンス独特のサービスを提供する人気ホテルとなっている。

Records show that the tiny mountaintop village of Saint-Paul-de-Vence was settled as early as 1016. Today the population is still only 2,000, and the village retains much its quaint medieval appearance. The facade of the hotel, Le Saint-Paul, was originally built in the sixteenth century.

The hotel first opened in June 1989, but it was bought by its present owner in 1991 and completely renovated. It now has nineteen guest rooms, with Provence-style interiors covered in "Souleïdo" fabric, a product unique to the region. During the renovation the owners also added a restaurant, one wall of which is painted with a trompe-l'oeil courtyard and garden. Although the hotel opened only recently, the warm Provençal-style service provided by its staff of twenty has already made it popular with guests.

1,3: 国王フランソワ1世（在位1515～1547年／1449～1547年）時代の1536年に村の基礎が完成したと伝えられるサン・ポール・ド・ヴァンス。1950年代に撮影された村の写真と現在（写真提供：ル・サン・ポール）。2: ホテルのロゴ・マークは村を描いたもの。4: ホテルの地下2階部分に設けられた屋外の「テラス」レストラン。最大22席。ホテルは城壁で囲まれた村の南側に位置する。

1, 3: The foundation for the village of Saint-Paul-de-Vence was completed in 1536 during the era of King François I (1449–1547; reigned 1515–1547). The village as it appeared in the 1950s, and today (photos courtesy of Le Saint-Paul). 2: A painting of the village is incorporated in the hotel's logo. 4: The outdoor *Terrasse* restaurant, on the second basement level, has seating for 22. The village is surrounded by castle walls, with the hotel on the south side.

5,6: 1930年代に撮影されたポストカード（ポストカード提供：ル・サン・ポール）。現在ここはホテル入口として使われている。かつてのサン・ポール・ド・ヴァンスは職人と芸術家の村として知られ、画家のマティス、ピカソが一時滞在。画家シャガールが晩年ここで暮らし彼の墓もあることから、コート・ダジュールの観光名所のポイントとなっている。7: ホテル・マネージャーのジョアンナ、ヤン・ゼット夫妻。ジョアンナは以前カンヌのホテル・マルチネスに勤務。ヤンはプルマン・ソフィア・カントリー・クラブの客室マネージャーを務め、1992年から現職。8: この村はニース国際空港から15kmの距離にある。9:「レセプション」のスタッフ。10: 白い漆喰天井と壁でコーディネートされた「レセプション」。11: ホテル1階の平面図。

5, 6: A postcard from the 1930s showing what is now the hotel entrance (postcard courtesy of Le Saint-Paul). Saint-Paul-de-Vence was known as a village of craftsmen and artists, and it was a temporary home for both Henri Matisse and Pablo Picasso. Marc Chagall spent his later years here and is also buried here, making the village a local Côte d'Azur sightseeing spot. 7: Hotel managers Joanna and Yann Zedde. Joanna Zedde worked at the Hotel Martinez in Cannes, while Yann worked as guest room manager at the Pullman Sophia Country Club before starting here in 1992. 8: The village is 15 kilometers from Nice International Airport. 9: The *Reception* staff. 10: The *Reception* area has white plaster walls and ceiling. 11: A floor plan of the ground floor and basement levels.

10

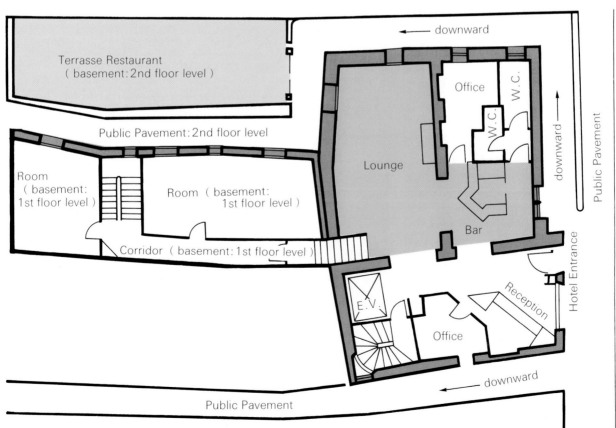

Terrasse Restaurant
(basement : 2nd floor level)

downward

Office

W.C.

W.C.

Public Pavement : 2nd floor level

Public Pavement

Room
(basement :
1st floor level)

Room (basement :
1st floor level)

Lounge

downward

Corridor (basement : 1st floor level)

Bar

E.V.

Reception

Hotel Entrance

Office

downward

Public Pavement

11

12

12-14:「レセプション」と「ラウンジ」の間に置かれた「バー」。13: メートル・ドテルのA・フェラリーニ。15: このホテルのオーナー、オリヴィエ・ボルロー。ボルローは世界40カ国、411カ所のホテルとレストランが加盟するルリ・エ・シャトー・ホテル協会本部の総支配人を5年間務めた実績をもつ。彼のこのホテルに対する経営哲学は5つのC（特徴、丁寧さ、落ちつき、魅力、料理）から成る。16-18: 暖炉とクラシックな食器棚を置いた「ラウンジ」。暖炉上の絵は19世紀に描かれたもの。18: 本棚中央

の絵は1751年に描かれた。この「ラウンジ」はロビー・バーとして機能する。

12–14: The *Bar* stands between the *Reception* and *Lounge* areas. 13: Maître d'Hôtel Alessandro Ferrarinni. 15: Hotel owner Olivier Borloo. Borloo has worked for five years as General Manager of Relais & Château Hotel Association, which has a total of 411 participating hotels and restaurants in 40 countries. He sums

up his management philosophy here as the "five C's"—Character, Courtesy, Calm, Charm and Cuisine. 16–18: The *Lounge* has a fireplace and an old-fashioned buffet cabinet. The painting above the fireplace dates back to the nineteenth century. 18: The painting in the middle of the bookshelves was painted in 1751. The *Lounge* also serves as the lobby bar.

13

14

15

16

17

18

19 20

21

19-26,29,30: 1993年4月、増設・改装され2
カ所のエリアから成る「ル・サン・ポール」レストラ
ン。ここは地下2階部分に位置し、外に設けられた
「テラス」レストラン（写真:26）に直接出られる設計
が取り入れられている。壁下部のバラストレイド（石の
手摺）、壁中部の花園と風景画はプロヴァンス風 "ト
ロンプ・ルイユ（だまし絵）"と呼ばれる。壁中央を飾
る石造りの壁噴水は16世紀製。

19–26, 29, 30: *Le Saint-Paul* restaurant was
redecorated and enlarged to two sections in
April 1993. It is on the second basement level
and connects directly with the outdoor *Terrasse*
restaurant (photo no. 26): The balustrade on the
lower part of the wall and the garden and scenic
view above are a Provence-style "trompe-l'œil"
painting. The stone fountain in the middle of the
wall dates back to the sixteenth century.

22

23

24

25

26

27

28

22: 小鴨のロースト、野菜と長カボチャの花添え。
23: あんこうのメダリヨン、野菜詰め長カボチャ添え。24: イトヨリのホウレンソウ包み、トマト・サフラン添え。25: 若い総料理長のジャッキー・レナールとスタッフ。レナールはブルターニュ生まれの26歳。スイス・ローザンヌの「レストラン・アゴラ」で修業、フランス・ブラントームのミシュラン一つ星をもつ「ムーラン・ドラベイ」の料理長C・ラヴィネルのアシスタントを務め1992年から現職。27,28:「ル・サンポール」レストランの横に新装された朝食専用のレストラン。29,30:「ル・サン・ポール」レストランの食器はレノーのリモージュ焼。食器のデザインは、1790年製〝ラファイエット〟と呼ばれるもの。このデザインはオリジナルの皿を所有するルーヴル美術館の許可を

得て製作された。グラスにもロゴ・マークが印刷されている。

22: Roast duck with olives, served with vegetables and zucchini flowers (*caneton rôti aux olives, petits légumes en tapenade, sa cuisse en fleur de courgette*). 23: Monkfish flavored with anise, served with stuffed zucchini (*medaillons de lotte à l'anis et ses petits farcis de courgettes*). 24: Red mullet with saffron-flavored tomato and fresh spinach (*rosace de rouget de roche à la tomate safranée, épinards frais*). 25: The young Chef de Cuisine Jackie Renard and his staff. Renard is 26 years old, and was born in Bretagne. He trained at the *Restau-*

rant Agora in Lausanne, Switzerland, then worked as assistant to Chef Christian Ravinel at the Michelin one-star restaurant *Moulin de l'Abbaye* in Brantôme, France, before coming here in 1992. 27, 28: Next to *Le Saint-Paul* restaurant is a newly decorated breakfast restaurant. 29, 30: Servingware at *Le Saint-Paul* is Limoges china by Reynaud. The "Lafayette" design was created in 1790. The original plate with this design is in the Louvre Museum, which gave its permission for the design to be used here. The Hotel's Logo mark is etched into the glassware.

29

30

31

32

33

34

35

31: 花をデザインしたブルーの共布でベッドカバーとカーテンをコーディネートしたスタンダードの部屋「22号室」。32:「ジュニア・スイート(20号室)」の応接間。33,36: スタンダードの部屋「29号室」。ベッド・ダウン時には全室にミネラルウォーターが2本サービスされる。34: スタンダードの部屋「38号室」。35: 大きなバルコニーを付設した「テラス・スイート(30号室)」。写真は朝食のセッティング。37: スタンダードの部屋「27号室」の浴室。38: 1840年製のアンティーク・デスクが置かれるスタンダード

の部屋「28号室」。このホテルには計19室(スイート3室含む)が設けられている。

31: Bedspreads and curtains in *Room 22*, a standard guest room, use matching floral-patterned blue fabric. 32: The sitting room of the *Junior Suite (Room 20)*. 33, 36: *Room 29*, a standard guest room. Two bottles of mineral water are delivered to each room when the beds are turned down. 34: *Room 38*, a stand-

ard room. 35: The *Terrasse Suite (Room 30)* includes a large balcony. The photo shows a breakfast setting. 37: The bathroom of *Room 27*, a standard guest room. 38: *Room 28*, a standard room, with an antique desk from 1840. The hotel has 19 guest rooms, including three suites.

36

37

38

39

40

41

42

43

44

45

39–45: 竹製の天蓋ベッドを設けたスタンダードの部屋「35号室」。39, 40: 暖かい木の温もりを感じさせるトイレット・ペーパー・ホルダーとヴィクトリア様式のバスタブ蛇口。41, 42: 浴室の備品とアニック・グタル製バス・アメニテイ。43: 部屋からの眺望。44: ドア裏の衣服掛け金具。1989年、ホテルとして開業した際使われていたインテリアは現在のオーナーが取得した1991年以降全てかえられた。その中でも総てのファブリック・デザインはプロヴァンス様式"スーレアドォ"と呼ばれ、この地域独特なもの。このホテルは、谷を眺望する部屋（スタンダード、ジュニア・スイート、テラス・スイート）に少し高めの料金が設定されている。

39–45: *Room 35*, a standard room furnished with a bamboo-canopied bed. 39, 40: A wooden toilet paper holder with a warm, natural feeling, and an old-fashioned Victorian-style bathtub faucet. 41, 42: Bathroom facilities, and bath amenities supplied by Annick Goutal. 43: A view from the room. 44: A clothes hanger on the back of the door. The hotel originally opened in 1989, but the interiors of all the rooms were completely changed in 1991 when it was bought by the present owner. The interiors are done in Provençal "Souleïado" fabrics unique to this region. Rooms with a view of the valley (Standard, Junior Suite and Terrasse Suite) are slightly more expensive than other rooms.

Hotel Royal Riviera

3, Avenue Jean Monnet, 06230 Saint-Jean-Cap-Ferrat, France

大都市リゾートのカンヌやニースとは趣を異にする小さな町ボーリューの西海岸（フェラ岬の付け根）に開発されたホテルである。開業は1905年。最初の名称はパノラマ・パレス・ホテルとしてスタート。この時、裏に同経営のホテル・サヴォワも建設された。建築家はニースのC・ルグレル。開業時のホテルはプライヴェート・ビーチに設けられたガレージから直接モーター・ボート遊びが楽しめる画期的な設計により、避寒に訪れる多くのイギリス人ゲストに愛用されたという。その後、アパートメントを備えたホテル・ベッドフォードと改名され、ホテル・サヴォワと共にベール家が1972年まで所有した。

1985年、ソシエテ・ベッドフォード・ホールディング社に所有権を譲渡。1987年からホテル・ファサードを残し内部のリノヴェーションが約24億円をかけて行なわれた。1989年4月、シックな新ホテルとして見事に再開業をはたしている。

The Hotel Royal Riviera sits at the base of a cape along the western shore of Beaulieu-sur-Mer, a small town with a very different atmosphere from the large resort cities of Cannes and Nice. The hotel first opened in 1905 as the Panorama Palace Hotel, designed by local Nice architect C. Legresle. The Hotel Savoy was built directly behind it, and opened at the same time and under the same management. During that era the hotel drew a large number of guests from England, who came to escape the cold winters there. One modern feature that appealed to guests was the availability of motorboats for recreational use; the hotel had a private beach with its own motorboat garages. The Berrut family owned the hotel and the nearby Hotel Savoy until 1972; at one point the Panorama Palace was converted to an apartment hotel and its name was changed to the Hotel Bedford.

In 1985 ownership was transferred to the Société Bedford Holding Company, and renovation work began in 1987, during which the interiors were completely redone and the original facade was restored at a total cost of 80 million French francs. In April 1989 a chic new hotel reopened for business.

1: 1906年に投函されたポストカード。中央左が現在のホテル。この時代の名称はパノラマ・パレス・ホテル（ポストカード提供：ホテル・ロイヤル・リヴィエラ）。2: 入口の鉄製装飾庇。3: 庭園と屋外プールを望むテラスに設けられたレストラン「ラ・テラス」。ここは夏季のメイン・レストランとして使われ、プールサイドにレストラン「ラ・パーゴラ（蔓棚）」が夏季のみオープンする。

1: A postcard from 1906. The hotel, then called the Panorama Palace Hotel, is at center left (postcard courtesy of Hotel Royal Riviera). 2: A decorative iron canopy covers the entrance. 3: The terrace at restaurant *La Terrasse* looks out over the garden and outdoor pool. *La Terrasse* is used as the main dining room during the summer months, and the summer-only poolside restaurant *La Pergola* is also open.

4

7

BEAULIEU-SUR-MER
PANORAMA-PALACE-HOTEL

5

6

8

4: 現在の国道（N-7）から眺望するボーリューの町とフェラ岬。1930年頃撮影された写真。フェラ岬の左側付け根にある建物がホテル。その右側に同経営のホテル・サヴォワ（現在は壊されている）が見える。5: 1906年に投函されたポストカード。6: 開業時のホテルを描いたイラスト。イラスト右下にモーターボート用ガレージが見える。7: ホテルのロゴ・マークを刻んだ真鍮製キー・ホルダーとキー。9: ベルマンの帽子。10: 開業時のデザインを残した階段室。手摺子は鉄製。11: 1931年に投函されたポストカード。この時代、ホテルは改名されホテル・ベッドフォードと呼ばれた。12,13: 海岸の道路から撮影された1910年代の写真とほぼ同位地から撮影した現在のホテル（5-7,12,13の写真・ポストカード提供：ホテル・ロイヤル・リヴィエラ）。テラスにガラス張りのレストラン「ル・パノラマ」が1989年設けられた。8,14: フランス様式の庭園から見たホテル全景。開業時のファサードが保存されている。

HOTEL PANORAMA PALACE
ST JEAN SUR MER

9

10

11

12

13

14

4: A photo from around 1930 shows the town of Beaulieu-sur-Mer and the cape seen from the site of the present national highway (N-7). At the base of the cape, on the left side, is the hotel building. To the right of that is the Hotel Savoy (now demolished), which was under the same management. **5:** A postcard from 1906. **6:** A painting of the hotel around the time it opened. To the lower right is the motorboat garage. **7:** A brass keyholder, engraved with the hotel logo, and a key. **9:** A bellman's cap. **10:** The original staircase, with iron banisters, has been preserved. **11:** A postcard from 1931, during the Hotel Bedford era. **12, 13:** The hotel, viewed from approximately the same spot along the shore road during the 1910s and at present (photos and postcards 5–7, 12 and 13 courtesy of Hotel Royal Riviera). The glass-enclosed restaurant *Le Panorama* was added in 1989. **8, 14:** A view from the French-style garden. The hotel's original façade has been preserved.

15

18

16

17

19

15: ホテルのシンボル・カラーであるブルーのユニフォームを着たベルマンとポーター。16: ヨーロッパでも珍しい女性コンシェルジュとチーフ・コンシェルジュのG・ペリモン。ペリモンはスイスのボー・リヴァージュ・パレス（ローザンヌ）、メリディアン（パリ）、プラザ・アテネ（パリ）を経て現職。17:「レセプション」のスタッフ。18: ホテルの入口の夜景。19: 総支配人ジルベール・イロンデル。スイスのローザンヌ・ホテル学校を卒業後、ホテル・ル・リシュモン（ジュネーヴ）、ホテル・ド・クリヨン（パリ）などを経て1990年7月から現職。20: イオニア式円柱と大理石の床でコーディネートされた「ラウンジ」。写真左側が「レセプション」、右側が庭園の出入口として使われるガラス・ドア。

15: The hotel's own distinctive shade of blue is used for the uniforms of the bellmen and porter. 16: A female concierge (unusual even in Europe) and head concierge Georges Perrimond. Perrimond worked at the Beau-Rivage Palace (Lausanne), the Meridien (Paris), and the Plaza Athenée (Paris) before coming here. 17: *Reception* staff. 18: The entrance at night. 19: General Manager Gilbert Irondelle. After graduating from Lausanne Hotel School Irondelle worked at Hotel Le Richemond (Geneva) and Hotel de Crillon (Paris) before starting here in July 1990. 20: The *Lounge*, with marble floors and Ionic columns. To the left of the photo is the *Reception* area, and to the right is a glass door leading to the garden.

21

22

23

24

21：5カ所置かれているサロンの中で最大の「サロン・メディテレネ（地中海）」。7×14m、98㎡。カクテル形式で150名、バンケット形式で100名を収容する。写真はスクール・ミーティング形式のセッティング。22：庭園側に設けられた「サロン・リヴィエラ」。6×10m、60㎡。カクテル形式で約70名、バンケット形式で約40名を収容する。23-25：「ラウンジ」の横に接続する「バー・ル・ベッドフォード」。テラスを付設する。23：チーフ・バーマンのA・ビィヨニション。24：「バー・ル・ベッドフォード」入口に飾られるペイストリー類。「ラウンジ」で楽しむティーのサービスはバー・スタッフが担当する。25：濃いブルーの壁、チェック柄の茶色のカーテンで飾られた「バー・ル・ベッドフォード」の内部。26：1階の平面図。

21: The *Salon Mediterranée*, the largest of five salons, measures 7 by 14 meters (22 by 45 feet), for a total area of 98 square meters (1,044 square feet). It has a capacity of 150 persons for cocktail parties, and 100 for banquets. In the photo, the room is set up for a "school meeting." 22: The *Salon Riviera*, on the garden side, measures 6 by 10 meters (19 by 32 feet), with an area of 60 square meters (639 square feet) and a capacity of 70 persons for cocktails and 40 for banquet-style events. 23–25: *Bar Le Bedford* is next to the *Lounge*, and includes a terrace. 23: Head barman Alain Burnichon. 24: A selection of pastries is on display at the entrance to *Bar Le Bedford*. The bar staff also serves tea in the *Lounge*.25: The interior of *Bar Le Bedford* has dark blue walls and brown checkered curtains. 26: A floor plan of the ground floor.

25

Road

Hotel Entrance

Car park

Office | Office | Office | Office | E.V. | Reception

Office | Kitchen

Salon Mediterranée

Restaurant Le Panorama

Pavement

Corridor

Corridor

Bar Bedford

Lounge

Salon du Cap

Salon Riviera

Salon Azur

Terrasse of Bar Bedford

Restaurant La Terrasse

Green

Garden

Pool

Restaurant La Pargola

Bar Piscine

26

27

28

29

30

31

32

27-34: ボーリューの町やビーチを望む、その名も
レストラン「ル・パノラマ」。60席。開業時のホテル名
称が使われる。27: サーモンときゅうりのタルタル
風。28: 薫製サーモンの背肉、酢づけアスパラガス
添え。29: 仔牛の焼肉・セージ風、バリグール（きの
この一種）添え。30: かりっとした鯛と野菜、めぼう
きとオリーヴのソース。31: イチゴのティヤン。プロ
ヴァンス地方の素焼きの容器を模した形状からこの
名がある。32: レストラン・ディレクター（中央）のF・
コンルーとスタッフ。33: テラスにつくられたレストラ
ン「ル・パノラマ」。34: 総料理長のイヴ・マーヴィル
とスタッフ。マーヴィルはフランスのグランド・ホテル・
ド・ラ・レーヌ（ナンシー）でスー・シェフ、1988年セ
イシェルのホテル・メリディアンで総料理長に就任。
1990年3月から現職。

27-34: A view of the town of Beaulieu-sur-Mer
and the beach from the appropriately named
restaurant *Le Panorama*. The restaurant seats
60, and takes its name from the original name of
the hotel. 27: Fresh salmon and cucumber
cream, Tartar style (*tartare de saumon frais aux
condiments crème de concombre*). 28:
Smoked salmon back and asparagus tips in
sour cream (*dos de saumon balik fumé à la
façon des tsars, pointes d'asperges et crème
acidulée*). 29: Roast filet of baby lamb with
sage, served with artichokes and dried tomatoes (*filet d'agnelet rôti aux senteurs de sauge,
barigoule d'artichauts violets et tomates
séchées*). 30: Crisp skin of sea bream with basil
oil and assorted vegetables (*dauradine peau
croustillante huile de basilic et multicolore de

légumes*). 31: Fruit *tian* flavored with tea (*tian de
fruits éxotiques au parfum des thés*). A *tian* is a
shallow casserole dish used in Provence. 32:
Director of Restaurants Fabrice Conroux (center) and staff. 33: Restaurant *Le Panorama* was
built on the terrace. 34: Chef de Cuisine Yves
Merville and staff. Merville worked at the Grand
Hotel de la Reine (Nancy), and in 1988 was
head chef at the Hotel Meridien (Seychelles)
before starting here in March 1990.

33

34

35

36

37

38

39

40

41

42

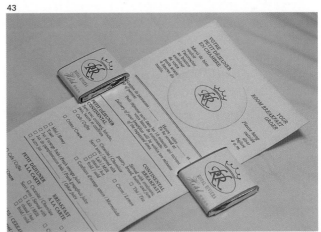

43

35,41-43: 眺望が素晴らしい建物のコーナーに置かれた「スイート(416号室)」。プライヴェート・ロビー、シッティング・スペースを設けた寝室、浴室から構成される。36: 庭園に面したスタンダードの部屋「110号室」は大きなバルコニーを付設する。37: ルームサービスで運ばれた朝食のセッティング。38: バス・アメニテイ。39,40: ハウスキーパーのスーパーバイザーとスタッフ。42: プール・エリアの写真が使われるマッチ。43: 朝食用ドアタッグ。ホテルには計77室(スイート5室含む)の部屋が設けられ、ボーリュー駅から1km、ニース国際空港から18kmの距離に位置する。また、新方式のスパ・センターが現在建設中である。

35, 41–43: *Suite 416* is a corner suite, and offers guests a fabulous view. It contains a private lobby, a bedroom with sitting area, and a bathroom. **36**: *Room 110*, a standard room facing the garden, includes a large balcony. **37**: A room service breakfast. **38**: Bath amenities. **39, 40**: The housekeeping supervisor and staff. **42**: A photo of the pool area appears on the matchboxes. **43**: A door tag for ordering breakfast. The hotel has a total of 77 guest rooms (including five suites), and is situated 1 kilometer from Beaulieu train station and 18 kilometers from Nice International Airport. A new Spa Center is now under construction at the hotel.

44 45

46 47

44: ホテルの夜景。45,47: 部屋のバルコニーから望むプール・エリア。白いテント屋根内部には、夏季のみのレストラン「ラ・パーゴラ（蔓棚）」と「バー・ピシーヌ」が設けられ、バーベキューが楽しめる。この期間（夏季）レストラン「ル・パノラマ」は閉められ、レストラン「ラ・テラス」がメイン・ダイニングとして使われる。46: 噴水を置いた庭園の花壇には、ホテルの頭文字（R.R.）が花でデザインされている。

44: A nighttime view of the hotel. 45, 47: The pool area, seen from one of the guest room balconies. Under the white tent-style roof are the *Bar Piscine* and the summer-only restaurant *La Pergola*, where guests can enjoy a nightly barbecue. During the summer months *Le Panorama* restaurant is closed, and *La Terrasse* restaurant serves as the main dining room. 46: The hotel's initials (R.R.) are formed by flowers in the garden, which also contains a fountain.

Hotel Bel-Air Cap-Ferrat

71, Bd du Gal-de-Gaulle, 06290 Saint-Jean-Cap-Ferrat, France

20世紀の初めにベルギー王レオポルド2世の冬のヴィラ・レジデンスがフェラ岬に建てられたことから、この地域の開発が始まった。さらにこの時、史上初めての〝自動車トゥーリズムの時代〟が到来、オテリエー・ド・サントル・ド・トゥーリズム・オートモビル社により岬の突端にホテルが建設されることになった。開業は1908年。最初の名称はグランド・ホテル・デュ・キャップ・フェラ。第1次世界大戦まではロシア皇室に度々使われ、その後フランス大統領だったP・デシャネルやティテュレスコ、アーガイル公爵夫人（ヴィクトリア女王の王女）、コンノート公爵がホテルに集い、第2次世界大戦前までの期間、ここは華麗なホテルとして名を高めた。

その後、1986年から5年間をかけてホテル内部が改装され、地中海を見渡す思いもかけない屋外プールをホテルの崖下に新設した。6ヘクタールの敷地に建つ白い外装の小型ホテルとして世界中のゲストを魅了している。

The Cape Ferrat area began developing at the start of the twentieth century when King Leopold II of Belgium built his winter villa residence here. It was also the dawn of the age of the automobile and automotive tourism, and in 1908 the Hotelière de Centre de Tourisme Automobile Company built a hotel at the tip of the cape, naming it the Grand Hotel du Cap Ferrat. The Russian royal family often stayed here before World War I, and in the years between the wars it was famous as an elegant gathering spot for such celebrities as French President Paul Deschanel, Titulesco, the Duchess of Argyll (Queen Victoria's daughter) and the Duke of Connaught.

In 1986 the hotel began five years of renovation work, during which the interior was completely redecorated. An outdoor pool with a view of the Mediterranean was also built at the base of the hotel cliff. Today guests from around the world enjoy the charms of this small-scale white hotel and its vast six-hectare grounds.

1：開業2年後の1910年に使われたポストカード。この時代、庭園中央には歩道が設けられていなかった（ポストカード提供：ホテル・ベル・エアー・キャップ・フェラ）。現在もポストカードと同様のファサード・デザインが保存されている。2：ホテル入口。3：クラシック家具と近代的家具が使われる「エントランス・ホール」。写真左奥にキャッシャー専用の部屋が置かれている。

1: A postcard from 1910, two years after the hotel opened, when the walkway at the center of the garden was not yet complete (postcard courtesy of Hotel Bel-Air Cap-Ferrat). The original façade still exists today. 2: The hotel entrance. 3: The *Entrance Hall* mixes old-fashioned and modern styles of furniture. At the far left is the cashier's room.

4

5

6

7

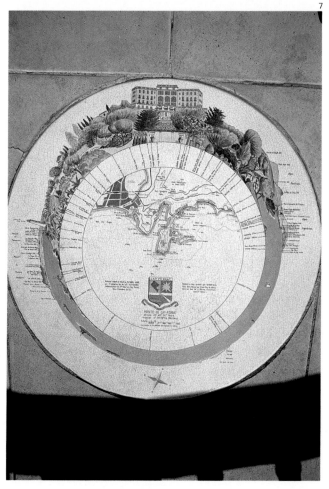

8

9

4: テニスコートに通じる階段上部から見たホテル
入口側のファサード。5: 開業時のポスター。ファサ
ードの前と後ろが逆に描かれた珍しい作品（ポスタ
ー提供：J・クロード・ギィヨン＝総料理長）。6: 数百
種類の草花で整えられた庭園から見たホテル。7:
展望台の床に埋め込まれているホテルとフェラ岬
の方位案内地図。8: 総支配人のハンスヨルグ・マ
イセン。1945年スイス生まれ。1968年ホテル・デ・
ベルグ（ジュネーヴ）を振り出しに、1983年レドラ・
マリオット・ホテル（アテネ）を経て現職。9, 13: 3台
用意されているリムジンのひとつ。ニース国際空港
や駅からの送迎に使われる。10: ホテル1階の平
面図と断面図。

4: The entrance-side façade, seen from the top
of the steps leading to the tennis courts. 5: An
unusual poster dating from the hotel's opening,
in which the front and back façades are
reversed (poster courtesy of Chef de Cuisine
Jean-Claude Guillon). 6: The hotel seen from
the garden, where several hundred varieties of
flowers have been planted. 7: A guide map of
the hotel and the Cape Ferrat area is embedded
in the floor of the observation area. 8: General
Manager Hansjörg Maissen. Maissen was born
in Switzerland in 1945, and began his career at
the Hotel des Bergues (Geneva) in 1968 before
moving to the Ledra Marriott Hotel (Athens) in

1983. 9, 13: One of the hotel's three limousines,
used to transport guests to and from Nice International Airport and the local train station. 10: A
ground floor plan and sectional plan.

10

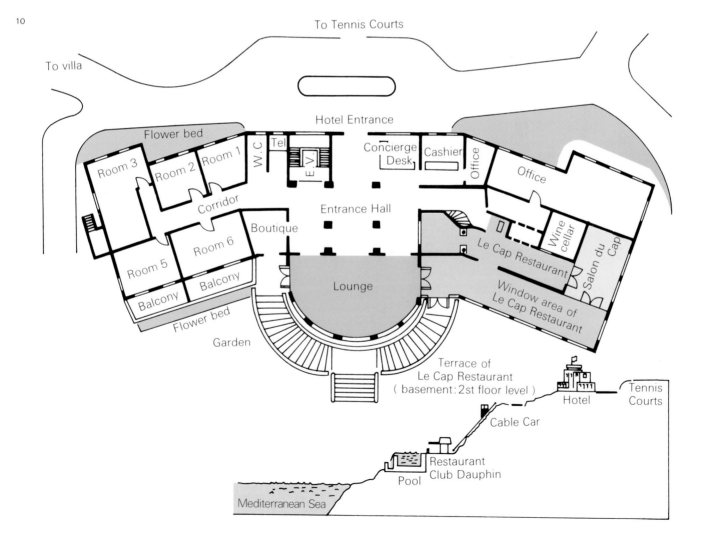

11

12

13

14

11: 入口の大窓を飾る鉄製装飾にはホテルの頭文字（F）がデザインされている。12:「エントランス・ホール」で使われるアンピール様式のシャンデリア。両翼を広げた白鳥の彫刻を照明部分のホルダーに多数使った珍しいもの。シャンデリア奥がシンボル・マークを飾った入口ドアの上部。14: 18年ホテルに勤務するミラノ生まれのチーフ・コンシェルジュ、M・ベルゼリーニ。15:「エントランス・ホール」で使われる鍍金スタンド・ランプのひとつ。16: レインボー・ストライプの布地を使ったモダン・チェアーのクッション。17,18:「エントランス・ホール」の横に位置する「ブティック」。「ブティック」を運営するのは総支配人夫人。

15

16

17

18

11: The hotel's initial ("F") is incorporated in the design of the iron ornaments on the large entrance window. 12: An unusual Empire-style chandelier in the *Entrance Hall*, with carved swans with outstretched wings beneath the lighting fixtures. Visible behind the chandelier is the top of the entrance door, decorated with the hotel's logo. 14: Milan-born chief concierge Mirko Berselline has been here 18 years. 15: One of the gilded floor lamps in the *Entrance Hall*. 16: A modern-style chair with rainbow-striped cushions. 17, 18: The *Boutique* next to the *Entrance Hall* is run by the wife of the hotel's general manager.

19　20

21

22

19,20:「エントランス・ホール」につながる「ラウンジ」。ここは庭園と地中海を望みながらお茶を楽しむ優雅なスペース。大窓を付設し、充分に太陽光を取り入れる半円形の設計。半円形の装飾ガラス天井、19世紀中期のものと思われるネオ・クラシック様式のアンティーク大鏡でコーディネートされている。21:「エントランス・ホール」で使われる英国ジョージ3世様式デザインを取り入れた鍍金コンソール・テーブル。22:「エントランス・ホール」中央に置かれた鍍金円形テーブル。台座にはイルカの彫刻が付けられている。このテーブルは19世紀初期に英国で多数つくられたデザインの複製品。

19, 20: Adjacent to the *Entrance Hall* is the *Lounge*, an elegant space where guests can enjoy tea while looking out over the garden and the Mediterranean Sea in the distance. The *Lounge* is semi-circular, with a decorative glass ceiling above and large windows on the sides to let in lots of sunlight. The area is filled with Neo-classic antique mirrors believed to date back to the mid-nineteenth century. 21: An English George III gilt console table stands in the *Entrance Hall*. 22: In the center of the *Entrance Hall* is a gilt circular table with carved dolphins on the pedestal. The table is a reproduction based on a design popular in England in the early nineteenth century.

23

23-27:「ラウンジ」の地下1階に位置する「ザ・サマーセット・モーム・ピアノ・バー」。貝殻を使った天井蛇腹、貝殻をフレームに飾った鏡、貝殻をディスプレイした置き物が階段を飾り、トロピカル・ムード溢れるバーである。28-31: 3カ所あるサロンのひとつ「サロン・デュ・キャップ」。5×10m、高さ4m、総面積50㎡。29: 木の葉をデザインしたカーテンと留め飾り房。30: アンティークの鍍金スタンド・ランプと円形小テーブル。もともと、この円形小テーブルは16世紀に燭台を置いたことからゲリドン（小円卓）と呼ばれる。31: コースター、ペン、ミーティング用の紙製フォルダーにもホテルのロゴ・マークが入れられている。

23-27: *The Somerset Maugham Piano Bar* is on the first basement level of the *Lounge*. The bar's tropical mood is reflected by the seashells decorating the ceiling cornice, the frames of the mirrors and the ornaments displayed along the stairway. 28-31: *Salon du Cap* is one of three salons, with a size of 5 by 10 meters (16 by 33 feet), a ceiling height of 4 meters (13 feet), and a total area of 50 square meters (528 square feet). 29: The curtains feature a tree-leaf design, and are held by a rope tassel tie-back. 30: An antique gilt floor lamp, and a small round table known as a *guéridon* (pedestal table). In the sixteenth century these tables were used as stands for candlesticks. 31: The hotel's logo appears on coasters, pens, and the paper folders supplied for meetings.

24

25

26

27

28

29

30

31

32

32-39: ミシュラン一つ星（1993年度）の「ル・キ
ャップ」美食レストラン。32: 地下2階部分には昼
食用の「テラス」が設けられている。椅子に座るの
が総料理長のジャン・クロード・ギィヨン。ギィヨンは
ストラスブールのホテル学校を卒業後、ロイヤル・ク
ラブ・エヴィアンなどを経て1961-1963年までフ
ランス海軍に勤務。1971年から現職。中央がファ
ースト・メートル・ドテルのJ・M・オウシイとスタッフ。
33,38:「ル・キャップ」美食レストランの壁ライトと
中央ダイニング・エリア。34,35,37,39:「ル・キ

ャップ」美食レストランの窓側エリアは魚や蟹を描い
たモザイク・タイル、孔雀やイルカなどを描いた壁画
で飾られている。36: ソムリエのD・デルカッセ。

32-39: *Le Cap* gourmet restaurant earned one
star in the Michelin Guide (1993 edition). 32:
The *Terrasse* luncheon restaurant is on the
second basement level. Seated in the chair is
Chef de Cuisine Jean-Claude Guillon. After
graduating from Strasbourg Hotel School, Guil-

lon worked at the Royal Club Evian, then did a
tour with the French Navy from 1961 to 1963. He
has been here since 1971. At center is first
maître d'hôtel Jean-Max Haussy and the restaurant staff. 33, 38: A wall light at *Le Cap*, and
the central dining area. 34, 35, 37, 39: Mosaic
tiles painted with fish and crabs and a fresco
painting of peacocks and dolphins decorate the
window-area wall of *Le Cap* gourmet restaurant.
36: Sommelier Daniel Delcassé.

33

34

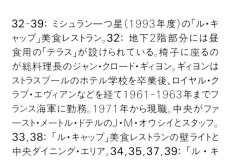

35

36

37

38

39

42

43

40

41

40-45: 総客室数59室(スイート11室含む)の中で最上階の5階海側に設けられた最高級の「スイート(403号室)」。40: ブロンズ製白鳥の置き物や馬をデザインしたコンソール・テーブルで飾られたプライヴェート・ロビー。左に寝室、右に応接間を配置する。41: 浴室のシンク部分。サウナを付設する。42,43: 大きなルーフ・ガーデンから望む庭園と地中海。直線歩道の突端、崖下に屋外プールがある。大きなルーフ・ガーデンは2カ所のエリアをもつ。44: 近代的デザインで飾られた応接間。ここは、写真右側の窓からルーフ・ガーデンへ出られる設計。45: ヘッドボードとベッドカバーを共布とした寝室。1986年のリノヴェーションで全ての部屋デザインがアメリカ式の近代的デザインに変えられた。

40-45: *Suite 403*, on the top (fourth) floor, is the most luxurious of the hotel's 59 guest rooms (including 11 suites). 40: A bronze swan ornament and a console table with a horse design decorate the suite's private lobby. The bedroom is to the left and the sitting room is to the right. 41: The bathroom's sink area. There is also a sauna attached. 42, 43: A view of the garden and the Mediterranean from the large roof garden. At the end of the pathway is the outdoor pool, at the base of the cliff. The roof garden is divided into two sections. 44: The modern sitting room. The roof garden can be reached through the window on the right. 45: In the bedroom, matching fabric is used for the bed's headboard and bedspreads. Modern, American-style interior design was introduced during the 1986 renovation.

44

45

46

46-52: ホテル4階中央部海側に3カ所設けられているスイートのひとつ「スイート（308号室）」。2本のエンタシス柱を設けた純白の広いバルコニーを付設。48: 庭園中央部から見たホテル。ホテル建物4階中央部に「スイート（308号室）」のバルコニーがある。49: ホテルのロゴ・マークを刻んだ真鍮製のキー・ホルダーとキー。50: 電話に設けられた各セクションへのダイレクト・コール・ボタン。万国共通のシンボル絵が印刷されている。51,52: バス・アメニテイと灰皿。53: 4階のエレヴェーター乗り場に置かれた鉄製のコンソール・テーブル。写真右側に設けられたエレヴェーターを階段が取り巻く設計。54: エレヴェーターは鉄製装飾ドアを開閉するクラシックなデザイン。

46-52: *Suite 308* is one of three suites facing the sea at the center of the third floor. The suite includes a spacious, sparkling white balcony with two entasis columns. 48: The hotel seen from the central portion of the garden. The balcony of *Suite 308* is visible at the center of the building's third floor (three stories above the ground floor). 49: A brass key holder, engraved with the hotel logo, and a key. 50: The telephones are marked with international communications symbols, and include direct call buttons for reaching each section of the hotel. 51, 52: Bath amenities, and an ashtray. 53: An iron console table in the third-floor elevator waiting area. The stairway winds around the elevator, visible to the right. 54: The elevator has an old-fashioned decorative iron door.

47

48

49

50

51

52

53

54

55

56

57

58

55-61：1986年から行なわれたリノヴェーション
でホテル崖下につくられた屋外海水プールとレスト
ラン「クラブ・ドファン（イルカ）」。ここには、庭園から
プールまでのケーブルカーも用意されている。56：
プールは海側の堰壁から、滝状に絶えず海水を流
す設計が取り入れられている。57：日光浴用のビ
ーチ・チェアーは3カ所に配置。58：4カ所（プール
下部）に点在する純白のテント生地を使ったカバー
ニャは、強烈な直射日光を避けるための小屋。59-
61：プール・サイドのレストラン「クラブ・ドファン」。
プロヴァンス地方料理やイタリア料理を提供する。
食器はリモージュ焼。熱で絵柄模様が変色しない
デコール・イナルテラブル。61：「クラブ・ドファン」マ
ネージャーのA・エルメンリッチ。夏にはプール・エリ
アでカクテル・パーティーも開かれる。5年間をかけ
たリノヴェーション（ホテル内部の改装とプール施
設の新設など）の総投資額は、当時の金額で60
億円を要した。

55–61: An outdoor pool and the restaurant *Club Dauphin* ('Dolphin') were constructed at the base of a cliff during the 1986 renovation. There is a cable car connecting the garden with the pool area. 56: Sea water flows continuously in a waterfall over the dam wall on the side facing the Mediterranean. 57: Beach chairs for sunbathing are available in three locations. 58: Four cabanas, covered with dazzling white tent fabric, are scattered around the lower end of the pool and provide respite from the fierce rays of the sun. 59–61: The poolside restaurant *Club Dauphin* serves Provençal and Italian-style cuisine. The servingware is heat-resistant *décor inaltérable* Limoges ware. 61: *Club Dauphin* Manager Alain Ellmenrich. The pool area is also the venue for cocktail parties in the summer. The five-year renovation project (during which the hotel interior was redecorated and the pool facilities were built) cost a total of US$25 million.

61

59

60

Château de la Chèvre d'Or

06360 Eze-Village, France

　ニースとモナコの中間、海岸から直接400mも立ち上がる岩山の山頂にあるエズ村のホテル。1924年、アメリカ人のヴァイオリニスト=ジョイスとスラート・バラコヴィッチ夫妻が廃墟同然だったエズ伯爵の城館跡に邸宅を築いたのがこのホテルのルーツ。夫妻が自らの手で建設した邸宅を〝黄金の山羊の館〟と呼んだことから、以来この名がホテルに使われている。1952年、夫妻はアメリカに帰国。翌年、邸宅を改装し同名の〝レストラン・ホテル〟として営業が開始された。その後、1990年には現在のオーナーが購入し、同時に村の2カ所のレストランも買収された。ホテルのレストラン「ラ・シェーヴル・ドール」はニースやフェラ岬の大パノラマを眺望するユニークな美食レストランとして人気が高い。

　この村の名称エズはフェニキア人の神イシス（イシア）に由来し、1036年頃から彼等の神殿が岩山に建てられていたことからこの名がある。

This hotel is located in the village of Eze, atop a 400-meter peak directly over the coastline between Nice and Monaco. The building was originally built by the American violinists Joyce and Slato Balakovitch, who constructed a private mansion for themselves on top of the ruins of the castle of Count Eze. The couple built their home with their own hands, and it was called the "House of the Golden Goat," after which the hotel took its name. In 1952 the Balakovitches returned to America, and the following year the mansion was redecorated and turned into a "restaurant hotel." In 1990 the hotel was purchased by its current owner, who also bought two restaurants in the village. The hotel's own gourmet restaurant, *La Chèvre d'Or*, is very popular for its "heavenly" panoramic view of Nice and Cape Ferrat.

Eze, the name of the village, is taken from the name of the Phoenician goddess Isis (or Isia); in the year 1036 a temple was built to the goddess on the mountaintop where the village now stands.

1： 1930年に撮影されたと思われるエズ村。時計塔や頂上に城閣跡を残す姿は現在と変わらない。写真左奥にホテルがある（写真提供：シャトー・ド・ラ・シェーヴル・ドール）。2： ホテル入口通路に吊られるロゴ・マークを記した鉄製看板。3： エズ村の公道でもあるホテル入口通路。4： フェラ岬の大パノラマを眺望するテラスに設けられた素晴らしい屋外プール。

1: A photo of the village of Eze, believed to be from 1930. The clock tower and the castle ruins still look the same today. The hotel building is in the left corner (photo courtesy of Château de la Chèvre d'Or). 2: An iron sign with the hotel's logo hangs over the entrance path. 3: The hotel entrance path is also a public thoroughfare of the village of Eze. 4: The outdoor pool has a terrace with a panoramic view of the cape.

5,7:「レセプション・ルーム」とレセプションのスタッフ。階段は美食レストラン「ラ・シェーヴル・ドール」へのアプローチ。6,8: 1992年の火災で新装された「ル・バー」。火災前ここには木調の食器棚、ピアノ、黄金の山羊像が置かれ、「ル・カクテル・ピアノ・バー」と呼ばれていた。9-11: 屋外プールを設けたテラスでは、朝食も提供される。燕尾服でサービスするメートル・ドテルのB・コズィモ。プール底にはホテルのロゴ・マークがタイルで組まれている。12: 左がアシスタント・マネージャーのS・トロイア、右が総支配人のT・ネイデュー。13: ホテル・オーナーのM・アラジ。14: 部屋の階段から見たテラス付近。ここは「ル・カフェ・デュ・ジャルダン（庭園のカフェ）」と呼ばれる。

5, 7: The *Reception Room* and its staff. The stairway leads to the gourmet restaurant *La Chèvre d'Or*. 6, 8: *Le Bar* was redecorated after a 1992 fire. Before the fire it was called *Le Cocktail Piano Bar* and was furnished with a wooden buffet cabinet, a piano and a statue of a golden goat. 9–11: Breakfast is served on the terrace of the outdoor pool. Service is provided by Maître d'Hôtel Bruno Cosimo, wearing a tailcoat. Colored tiles at the bottom of the pool form the hotel logo. 12: Assistant Manager Salvatore Troia (left) and General Manager Thierry Naidu (right). 13: Owner M. Harajchi. 14: The terrace area, seen from the guest room stairway. *Le Café du Jardin* is located here.

9

10

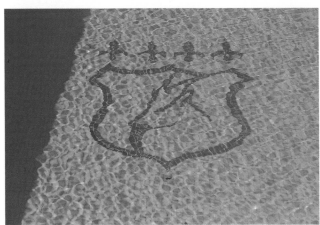

11

12

13

14

18

19

16

17

15-27: ミシュラン一つ星（1993年度）の美食レストラン「ラ・シェーヴル・ドール」。15: 長年、総料理長を務めるエリー・マゾとスタッフ。16,17: レストラン内部は暖炉を飾ったエリアと眺望を楽しむエリアに分かれている。18: ホテル・ロゴ・マーク入りのナプキン。19: レストランのサービス・スタッフ。中央左がソムリエのP・マニュー、中央右がメートル・ドテルのI・ラヴー。20: 仔兎のフォンダン、セロリとアーティチョーク添え。21: オマール・エビのサラダ。22: イトヨリのシュープレーム・赤ワイン・ソース、ズッキーニの花添え。23: 仔鳩のシュープレーム、トリュフ入り冷パスタ添え。24: パルフェと呼ばれるデザート。25: 黄金の山羊像と料理。26,27: 食器やグラスにもホテルのロゴ・マークが入れられている。食器はG・D・A社製のリモージュ焼、デコール・イナルテラブル。

15-27: *La Chèvre d'Or* gourmet restaurant earned one star in the Michelin Guide (1993 edition). 15: Longtime Chef de Cuisine Elie Mazot and his staff. 16, 17: The interior is divided into two sections, one with a fireplace and one with a panoramic view. 18: The hotel logo appears on the napkins. 19: The restaurant service staff. At center left is sommelier Philippe Magne, and at center right is Maître d'Hôtel Ivan Lavaux. 20: Fondant of young rabbit served with celery and artichokes (*fondant de lapereau, grecque de céleri et d' artichaut*). 21: Lobster salad with truffle oil (*homard bleu en salade à l'huile de truffes*). 22: Suprême of mullet with red wine sauce and zucchini flowers (*suprême de rougets en gastrique au vin rouge de Pibarnon*). 23: Suprême of squab with cold pasta and truffles (*suprême de pigeonneau aux pâtes fraiches enrobées de truffes*). 24: Liquorice parfait with chocolate and cherry juice (*parfait à la réglisse, en croustillant au chocolat guanda et jus aux griottes*). 25: A statue of a golden goat, and the restaurant's food. 26, 27: The hotel logo appears on the plates and glassware. Servingware is *décor inaltérable* Limoges china from the G.D.A. Company.

20

21

22

23

24

25

26

27

28

28-32: 計20室設けられている部屋の中で数室
設けられているコテージ形式の部屋「19号室」。ク
ラシックな暖炉、ルイ13世様式のフォートイユ(肘掛
け椅子)、ロングケース・クロックなどが使われてい
る。30: ホテルのロゴ・マークを刻んだ革製のキ
ー・ホルダーとキー。31,32: コテージ専用の屋外
プール。33-37: 専用のテラスを付設したコテージ

様式の部屋「38号室」。34-36: 浴室は近代的デ
ザイン。バス・アメニテイや枕にも山羊のロゴ・マーク
が入れられている。このホテルでは部屋を増設する
工事がゆっくりと進められている。尚、ホテル宿泊者
は、ホテルに隣接する2カ所のレストラン「ア・ヴォト
レーゼ」とレストラン「ル・グリル」がサインだけで利
用できる。

29

30

31

32

33

28–32: *Room 19* is one of several cottage-style rooms among the hotel's total of twenty guest rooms. The interior includes an old-fashioned fireplace, a Louis XIII *fauteuil* (upholstered armchair), and a Longcase clock. 30: A leather key holder, engraved with the hotel logo, and a key. 31, 32: An outdoor pool for guests staying in the cottages. 33–37: Cottage-style *Room 38* has its own terrace. 34–36: The bathroom is modern in design, and bath amenities and pillows bear the hotel logo. The hotel is now gradually adding more guest rooms. Hotel guests can sign their names and room numbers when dining at the two restaurants next to the hotel, *Restaurant à Vatoreze* and *Restaurant Le Grill*.

34

35

36

37

38

41

42

39

40

38: 1950年代のレストラン「ラ・シェーヴル・ドール」。39: 1920年代に撮影されたと思われるエズ村の写真。40: 1930年代に撮影された写真。現在のラゲット駐車場から撮影された写真と思われる。41,42: 1950年代後半にコート・ダジュールを襲った寒波で雪におおわれたプール付近と入口の通路。43,44: 1952～1953年に行なわれたホテルへの改築工事を記録した写真。45: 1957年、ホテルに滞在したウォルト・ディズニー。46: ホテルを訪れたモナコ王妃・故グレース・ケリーのスナップ（38-46の写真提供：シャトー・ド・ラ・シェーヴル・ドール）。47:「ル・バー」の出入口から眺望する屋外プールとキャップ岬の夜景。コート・ダジュールでも珍しい、海から直接400mも立ち上がる岩上に位置する、このホテルならではの絶景である。

38: La Chèvre d'Or restaurant in the 1950s. 39: The village of Eze in a photo believed to be from 1920. 40: A photo from the 1930s, probably taken from the site of the present Laghet parking area. 41, 42: The pool area and entrance road, covered by snow during a cold wave in the late 1950s. 43, 44: The reconstruction work of 1952-53 is commemorated in these photos. 45: Walt Disney, who stayed here in 1957. 46: A snapshot of Queen Grace of Monaco (Grace Kelly), who stayed at the hotel (photos 38-46 courtesy of Château de la Chèvre d'Or). 47: A view of the outdoor pool and the cape from the entrance to Le Bar. The hotel, standing 400 meters above the coastline, enjoys views that are spectacular even by Côte d'Azur standards.

43

44

45

46

47

Hotel Directory

Hotel Negresco
37, Promenade des Anglais, BP 379,
06007 Nice Cedex, France
Tel: (33)93 88 39 51   Fax: (33)93 88 35 68
Summary of hotel facilities
Total guest rooms: 140 (including 18 suites)
Restaurants: 2
Bars, Lounges: 2
Banquet・Meeting rooms: 4
Others: Shopping arcade
Affiliation, Reservations:
The Leading Hotels of the World
■施設概要
総客室数：140室（18スイート）
レストラン：2ヵ所
バー、ラウンジ：2ヵ所
宴会・集会施設：4ヵ所
その他：ショッピング・アーケード
■日本での予約・問い合わせ先
ザ・リーディングホテルズ・オブ・ザ・ワールド
〒102 東京都千代田区九段北3-2-2
Tel: (03)5210-5131   Fax: (03)5210-3805

Hotel Westminster Concorde
27, Promenade des Anglais,
06000 Nice, France
Tel: (33)93 88 29 44   Fax: (33)93 82 45 35
Summary of hotel facilities
Total guest rooms: 150 (including 15 suites)
Restaurants: 1
Bars, Lounges: 2
Banquet・Meeting rooms: 8
Others: Bar terrace, Restaurant terrace
Affiliation, Reservations:
Concorde Hotels
■施設概要
総客室数：150室（15スイート）
レストラン：1ヵ所
バー、ラウンジ：2ヵ所
宴会・集会施設：8ヵ所
その他：バー・テラス、レストラン・テラス
■日本での予約・問い合わせ先
コンコルド・ホテルズ
〒104 東京都中央区京橋2-11-6 弥生ビル5階
Tel: (03)3563-2621   Fax: (03)3563-2623

Hotel Martinez
73, La Croisette
06406 Cannes Cedex, France
Tel: (33)92 98 73 00   Fax: (33)93 39 67 82
Summary of hotel facilities
Total guest rooms: 430 (including 15 suites)
Restaurants: 2
Bars, Lounges: 2
Banquet・Meeting rooms: 12
Others: Le Restaurant de la Plage (summer only),
        Cannes Tennis Club, Private beach
Affiliation, Reservations:
Concorde Hotels
■施設概要
総客室数：430室（15スイート）
レストラン：2ヵ所
バー、ラウンジ：2ヵ所
宴会・集会施設：12ヵ所
その他：ル・レストラン・ド・ラ・プラージュ（夏期のみ）、
        カンヌ・テニス・クラブ、プライヴェート・ビーチ
■日本での予約・問い合わせ先
コンコルド・ホテルズ
〒104 東京都中央区京橋2-11-6 弥生ビル5階
Tel: (03)3563-2621   Fax: (03)3563-2623

Carlton Inter·Continental Cannes
58, La Croisette, PB 155,
06406 Cannes Cedex, France
Tel: (33)93 68 91 68   Fax: (33)93 38 20 90
Summary of hotel facilities
Total guest rooms: 355 (including 57 suites)
Restaurants: 3
Bars, Lounges: 3
Banquet・Meeting rooms: 11
Others: Carlton Casino Club, Private beach,
        Health center, Shopping arcade
Affiliation, Reservations:
Inter·Continental Hotels
■施設概要
総客室数：355室（57スイート）
レストラン：3ヵ所
バー、ラウンジ：3ヵ所
宴会・集会施設：11ヵ所
その他：カールトン・カジノ・クラブ、プライヴェート・ビーチ、
        ヘルス・センター、ショッピング・アーケード
■日本での予約・問い合わせ先
インターコンチネンタルホテルズ ジャパン㈱
〒106 東京都港区東麻布1-7-3 第2渡辺ビル7階
Tel: (03)5561-0701   Fax: (03)5561-0722
フリーダイヤル： 0120-455655

Le Château du Domaine Saint-Martin
Avenue des Templiers, 06140 Vence, France
Tel: (33)93 58 02 02   Fax: (33)93 24 08 91
Summary of hotel facilities
Total guest rooms: 25 (including 11 suites)
Restaurants: 1
Bars, Lounges: 2
Banquet・Meeting rooms: 3
Others: Tennis court, Outdoor pool, Helipord
        Open: April to October
Affiliation, Reservations:
Relais & Chateaux
■施設概要
総客室数：25室（11スイート）
レストラン：1ヵ所
バー、ラウンジ：2ヵ所
宴会・集会施設：3ヵ所
その他：テニス・コート、屋外プール、ヘリポート
        営業期間：4月～10月
■日本での問い合わせ先
ルレ・エ・シャトー日本事務局
〒104 東京都中央区銀座2-6-1
Tel: (03)3567-4834   Fax: (03)3567-4856

Le Saint-Paul
86, Rue Grande
06570 Saint-Paul-de-Vence, France
Tel: (33)93 32 65 25   Fax: (33)93 32 52 94
Summary of hotel facilities
Total guest rooms: 19 (including 3 suites)
Restaurants: 2
Bars, Lounges: 1
Banquet・Meeting rooms: 1
Others: Open: March through January
Affiliation, Reservations:
Relais & Chateaux
■施設概要
総客室数：19室（3スイート）
レストラン：2ヵ所
バー、ラウンジ：1ヵ所
宴会・集会施設：1ヵ所
その他：営業期間：3月～翌年1月
■日本での問い合わせ先
ルレ・エ・シャトー日本事務局
〒104 東京都中央区銀座2-6-1
Tel: (03)3567-4834   Fax: (03)3567-4856

Hotel Royal Riviera
3, Avenue Jean Monnet
06230 Saint-Jean-Cap-Ferrat, France
Tel: (33)93 01 20 20   Fax: (33)93 01 23 07
Summary of hotel facilities
Total guest rooms: 72 (including 5 suites)
Restaurants: 3
Bars, Lounges: 3
Banquet・Meeting rooms: 5
Others: Outdoor pool, Private beach, Spa Center
Affiliation, Reservations:
The Leading Hotels of the World
■施設概要
総客室数：72室（5スイート）
レストラン：3ヵ所
バー、ラウンジ：3ヵ所
宴会・集会施設：5ヵ所
その他：屋外プール、プライヴェート・ビーチ、
        スパ・センター
■日本での予約・問い合わせ先
ザ・リーディングホテルズ・オブ・ザ・ワールド
〒102 東京都千代田区九段北3-2-2
Tel: (03)5210-5131   Fax: (03)5210-3805

Hotel Bel-Air Cap-Ferrat
71, Boulevard du General-de-Gaulle,
06290 Saint-Jean-Cap-Ferrat, France
Tel: (33)93 76 50 50   Fax: (33)93 76 04 52
Summary of hotel facilities
Total guest rooms: 59 (including 11 suites)
Restaurants: 2
Bars, Lounges: 2
Banquet・Meeting rooms: 3
Others: Two Tennis courts, Outdoor pool
        Restaurant Terrace
Affiliation, Reservations:
Relais & Chateaux
■施設概要
総客室数：59室（11スイート）
レストラン：2ヵ所
バー、ラウンジ：2ヵ所
宴会・集会施設：3ヵ所
その他：テニス・コート（2面）、屋外プール、
        レストラン・テラス
■日本での問い合わせ先
ルレ・エ・シャトー日本事務局
〒104 東京都中央区銀座2-6-1
Tel: (03)3567-4834   Fax: (03)3567-4856

Château de la Chèvre d'Or
06360 Eze-Village, France
Tel: (33)93 41 12 12   Fax: (33)93 41 06 72
Summary of hotel facilities
Total guest rooms: 20 (including 6 suites)
Restaurants: 1
Bars, Lounges: 3
Banquet・Meeting rooms:
Others: Two outdoor pools,
        Two restaurants with same owner located
        nearby
        Open: April to December
Affiliation, Reservations:
Relais & Chateaux
■施設概要
総客室数：20室（6スイート）
レストラン：1ヵ所
バー、ラウンジ：3ヵ所
宴会・集会施設：1ヵ所
その他：屋外プール（2ヵ所）、隣接地に同経営のレストラ
        ン（2ヵ所）
        営業期間：4月～12月
■日本での問い合わせ先
ルレ・エ・シャトー日本事務局
〒104 東京都中央区銀座2-6-1
Tel: (03)3567-4834   Fax: (03)3567-4856

Profile

きしかわ ひろ とし
岸川惠俊

1951年、北海道小樽市生まれ。1972年より
ワールド・カップ・スキー・レース、国際自動車
ラリー・レースの記録映画、TV番組などのムー
ビー・カメラマンとして世界を廻る。1982年
からフォト・ジャーナリストに転向。以来、ライフ・
ワークとして世界のホテル取材を開始する。
年間6ヵ月を海外取材に費やし、1990年11月
までに世界の一流ホテル200余ヵ所を取材。
10年間の成果を収めた写真集「世界のホテ
ル(全6巻)」を世界のマーケットに向け、河出
書房新社より刊行。現在も究極のホテルを求
めて海外取材を継続中。また、日本商工会
議所「石垣」(87−90)、柴田書店「ホテル・
旅館」などの月刊誌に連載ページをもつ。企
業ポスター、カレンダーなどの広告メディアに
も多くの写真を提供。1987年度「日野自動車
カレンダー・世界の窓シリーズ」で全国カレン
ダー展入賞。1992年度「トステム・カレンダー」
などの作品がある。

連絡先:ケイ・プラニング
Tel:(03)3408-0288
Fax:(03)3478-3552

Hiro Kishikawa

Hiro Kishikawa was born in 1951 on
Japan's northernmost island of Hok-
kaido. In 1972 he began working as
a cameraman, traveling around the
world covering World Cup ski races,
international auto rallies and similar
events. In 1982 he switched to photography, specializing in international
hotels, and by November 1990, after
traveling six months of each year, he
had completed photo studies of some
200 first-class hotels around the world.
He is a regular contributor to several
monthly trade magazines in Japan, and
has also provided many photographs
for posters, calendars and other adver-
tising media, including a 1987 calendar
that won a prize in a Japanese nation-
wide calendar competition.

ひらしま じ ろう
平島二郎

1929年、東京に生まれる。54年、東京芸術大
学美術学部建築科卒業。61年、スペイン政
府名誉留学生に選ばれて渡西、美術学校
とマドリッド大学トローハ研究室に在籍する。
帰国後、東京芸術大学建築科講師を経て、
現在、平島建築設計事務所所長、山脇美
術専門学院理事長兼院長。東京芸術大学
の「カッパドキア中世キリスト教美術調査」に
参加し、また前記留学の前後をあわせて世
界47ヵ国を旅行した。クレッセント・ハウス、奥
志賀高原ホテル、葉山御用邸、赤坂御所内
東宮仮御所その他、多くの建築設計を手が
ける。著書に『世界建築史の旅』『リゾートホ
テルの開発計画』がある。

Jiro Hirashima

Jiro Hirashima was born in Tokyo in
1929, and in 1954 he graduated with
a degree in Architecture from the Fine
Arts Department of Tokyo National
University of Fine Arts and Music. In
1961 he was selected by the Spanish
government as an honorary exchange
student; in Spain he studied at the
School of Fine Arts and at the Torroja
Institute of the University of Madrid.
After returning to Japan he was a lec-
turer in the Architectural Department of
Tokyo National University of Fine Arts
and Music. Presently he is the head of
Hirashima Architectural Office as well
as the President and the Chairman of
the Board of directorate of the Yama-
waki Academy of Fine Arts. He was
a participant in Tokyo University of
Arts' "Cappadocia Survey of Medieval
Christian Art," and has traveled to a
total of 47 countries around the world.
He has handled architectural planning
for a large number of projects, including Crescent House, Okushiga Kogen
Hotel, the Hayama Imperial Villa and
the Temporary Palace of the Crown
Prince in the Akasaka Imperial Palace.
He has also written *Travels in World
Architectural History* and *Resort Hotel,
Development and Planning.*

SALLE DE RESTAURANT

A postcard from Le Grand Hotel (Nice), which no longer exists. Many of the Côte d'Azur's most beautiful hotels were either converted to apartment buildings or demolished, with only postcards and old photographs left behind.

VUE DU HALL

LE GRAND HOTEL

N MIDI
E LA VILLE
ARDIN

SALLE DES FÊTES

CLASSIC HOTELS OF THE WORLD: VOL.3

CÔTE D'AZUR

初版印刷　1994年6月20日
初版発行　1994年6月30日

写真・文　　岸川惠俊
監修　　　　平島二郎
デザイン　　有馬庸夫
翻訳　　　　ロブ・サターホワイト

発行者　　　清水　　勝
発行所　　　河出書房新社
　　　　　　〒151　東京都渋谷区千駄ヶ谷2-32-2
　　　　　　電話：(営業)03-3404-1201/(編集)03-3404-8611
　　　　　　振替：00100-7-10802

印刷　　　　大日本印刷株式会社
製本　　　　大口製本印刷株式会社

ISBN4-309-71593-1